Yuk's Fast Book

Yuk's Fast Book

by

Yuk Hodgson and Jonathan Pulleyn

© Yuk Hodgson and Jonathan Pulleyn, 2014

Published by JP Rallying Publications

www. yukspeed.com

The views expressed in this publication are the personal recollections of the authors and, in some cases, are referring to incidents which may have taken place up to 60 years ago. No offence is intended to any group or individual who may be mentioned.

A CIP catalogue record for this book is available from the British Library.

ISBN 978-0-9930854-0-6

Book layout and cover design by Clare Brayshaw

Prepared and printed by:

York Publishing Services Ltd
64 Hallfield Road
Layerthorpe
York YO31 7ZQ

Tel: 01904 431213

Website: www.yps-publishing.co.uk

Dedication

To my lovely daughter, Jem.

To my best friend, the late David 'Piggy' Thompson.

To my customers from all around the world and to all my good friends who I have made over the many years I have competed.

Thank you for buying the book!

Yuk's Acknowledgements

Special thanks to my buddy – 'JP' (Jonathan Pulleyn) for suggesting and putting this book together. We have had loads of laughs along the way working on this project mainly whilst pissed! Well – not JP – he hardly drinks!!

My thanks to everyone who supplied so many great photos for this book which I have collected over the years. I've not a clue where some of them come from, in fact most of them! But where possible we have given credits and made every effort to contact people to ask their permission.

Because some of these photos are really old, many people have moved on, but be assured we have done our best to seek permission where possible. Should we discover later that we have caused offence we shall make sure the proper accreditations are made in future editions... of which there are bound to be loads!

Also, thanks must go to all my friends who have contributed so many great stories for the book. We are both very grateful.

JP and I should also thank Duncan Beal and his team at YPS Publishing – for their patience and expertise publishing this book; we could not have done it without them!

JP's Acknowledgments

Thank you to Yuk for going along with my idea to produce this book. It was not exactly an original idea; people have been asking for one for years, but since Yuk and I live within a few miles of each other and have known each other for years it made sense for us to do it.

It has been enormous fun listening to Yuk's stories, but not always easy to keep him on track, mainly when he has had a drink! Well, one of us had to remain sober! The number of times he would say, "Where was I going with this, JP?", "What was the question?" or "Keep up, Jon!"

The stories just kept coming when we met up most weekends. *"How big a book do you want?"* he would say or *"ring Huddersfield Chris, he has loads of stories, but you will need about ten tapes!!!"*

I would get an email from him every now and then like this one:

"JP.....have found some folders of rally results in the 60s/70s.

Pop up and we'll have a rummage. Best bring 'young bucks', cos they are in the loft and it'll be dark.

Yuk"

I am not sure I believe all these stories myself. Some of them go back many, many years and they are bound to have changed! You will have to judge for yourself what is right and what wrong! One thing for sure, you will enjoy reading this if you are a true rally fan. Yuk is a real Yorkshire character and a fine story teller!

I must also thank the many fabulous contributions we have enjoyed from:

James Thompson, who kindly wrote the foreword
Bill Lumb
Christine Coward
Christine Oldfield
Chris Walker (Huddersfield Chris)
Craig Thorley
Dave Elcock (Billy Ballcock)
Dave Oldfield
Eddie Ganderton
Gavin Ruler (Fuzznag)
Ian Jemison (Wardrobe)
Ian Oldfield (Old Ianfield)
Jem Hodgson
John Forrest
Kevin Bardon (Billy Split Pin)
Lou Naylor
Mark (Skids) Skinner
Martin Welch
Mick Penrose (Super Mick)
Mike Greasley
Nigel Cay
Paul Skinner
Philip Welch
Steve Wilson (Animal)
Sue Lamb
Tony Coward
Tom Riordan (Guernsey Tom)

I have mixed the stories from the contributors in between Yuk's own personal stories. All the contributors' stories are shown in italics so you can tell the difference between their words and Yuk's. Also, any stories taken from previously published articles are also in italics. Many, many thanks to Motorsport News, Autosport and the York Press for their kind permission to reproduce certain articles.

Some of the great photographs from Yuk's collection do not have any record of who took them. However, we have had some great donations from:

Steve Pugh
Phill Andrews at www.rallyaround.co.uk
Fergus McAnallen at www.rallyretro.com
Jim Goodman
Tony Coward
Robert Griffin at www.rallyphotos.co.uk

I should also like to give very special thanks to Jim Goodman and Mike Nicholson for their valuable advice and experience, which helped make some important decisions when producing the book.

Finally, special thanks to my wife Kerry for helping me edit all the stories and my family for putting up with all the hours I spent at the laptop instead of being with them!

We hope you enjoy reading this as much as we enjoyed putting it together.

One thing is for sure, there is only one Yuk Hodgson..........

Thank Goodness!

Jonathan Pulleyn

Jonathan Pulleyn, better known by many as "JP" has been around clubman rallying for nearly as long as Yuk! He started his rally career in 1975 driving Minis (just like Yuk) in road and stage events with little success! He then moved on to Escorts (just like Yuk!) but the money soon ran out and he continued to compete by co-driving for many top local Yorkshire drivers in the 1980s such as Ian Oldfield, Ian Jemison and Dick Rowland and occasionally servicing or chasing for some local teams before leaving competition behind to concentrate on a career in newspapers then latterly management consultancy. He later returned to driving in various Gp. 4 Escorts between 2002 and 2006.

A true rally enthusiast, JP and Yuk have been friends for many years and share the passion for the sport. JP's knowledge of British rallying has made him a bit of a rallying anorak, particularly with regards to Ford Escorts, but don't tell anyone! Historic rally journalist, Paul Lawrence, called him the "Rally Escort Guru" which seems to have stuck with him now!

Contents

James Thompson

Foreword

I am proud to be asked to write a foreword for Yuk. He was my Dad's best friend. They had a fantastic relationship and such fun times, as you will read about in this book. There was always something going on. They were like two naughty school boys who had escaped from school for the day! Thick as thieves!

I have so many overwhelming memories and whenever I think of Yuk, I smile! There was always a massive sense of fun when he and my father got together and never, ever a dull moment!

I always wanted to be a World Rally Champion. I grew up with rallying all around me and of course you aspire to be like your father inside and outside the car. When I was really very young, we got a Mk. 2 Escort off Yuk which I could play with around the farm and occasionally we would go to the motor club monthly autotests, an ideal place to learn all about car control. I rarely got any great results on those events, as remembering the route often challenged me, but I always enjoyed doing the doughnuts and handbrake turns, though!

I wanted to earn a living rallying but there were so few opportunities, my Dad steered me towards circuit racing where many more works drives existed to make a living. It was the right choice of course and I have never regretted it.

I did get to try a few rallies in the early 2000s in the Peugeots and Mitsubishis with some pretty good successes in amongst the crashes! Yuk was usually there to witness them too! His job was to accompany me on these events whenever he could. I was going to say to look after me but more likely to lead me astray! His job title was Chief Entertainments Officer!

When Yuk told me of his intentions to put this book together with JP, I said, "tell all!" and he nearly has, but don't worry, any names which may incriminate have been removed, I am told! Enjoy the book, I know I will!

James Thompson
Son of the late Piggy Thompson.

James is currently competing in the World Touring Car Championship. He has twice been champion of the British Touring Car Championship (BTCC) in 2002/2004 and European Champion 2009/2010.

Most notable rallying achievement is 2nd in Gp. N in the Network Q in 2004.

2014

1 – I was born in a pub!

I was born on the 12th December 19.., well, you don't need to know that bit, at Gate Helmsley between York and Stamford Bridge at The Black Horse pub, which is now three cottages.

We left the pub when I was nine years of age and moved to my auntie's (my dad's sister) at Stamford Bridge. My dad had been the publican amongst all sorts of other things. He was an agricultural haulage driver with his own wagon and he had a mobile fish and chip van which he set on fire on a foggy Friday night at Norgate near where Fatty Simmo lived!!!

Cheeky chappy!

He had a mate with him, Bri Pearson, who is still alive today and he tells me, "We had a hell of a fuckin' job when we saw the chip fire had started," so they chucked a load of fat on top and parked at the top of the hill, jumps out and these gas bottles started going off! He says they had to go right into the field up near the railway line because these bottles were going off! If you go into Norgate now you can still see the scarred tree which took the blast when a bottle blew out of the van!

Anyway, my dad had to leave the pub 'cos my mam left him for an RAF bloke from Full Sutton Airfield. She ended up living in Cyprus for years. She died at the age of 92, would you believe!

The RAF lads used to come to Gate Helmsley Village Hall to the dances held there, then go on to my dad's pub after. Dad never closed when they were there. My dad used to keep a special wooden barrel for the RAF lads with an extra jug of water in it 'cos they would be that pissed before they got there and they wouldn't know any different!!!!!

It's not a particularly good thing your parents splitting up when you are that young. We didn't stay in touch much; we were not that close a family really.

So we moved in to my auntie's place; 'Miss Hodgson' 'cos she never got married – and we all lived together with my nan, my auntie, my older brother Paul and my dad in this big house in Stamford Bridge.

Eventually, my dad moved to York and was a taxi driver; my brother had left and got married and I was left at my auntie's. I was a real loose cannon when he was not around, I can tell you!

Anyway, eventually I moved to my dad's place in Fulford in York which was next to Mike Bailey's garage which used to service those old light blue 3-wheelers for the disabled. He used to have this bloody great heap of old false legs! I used to pinch them. I've got a pair in my shop now where the swallows nest in them! Great big stumps they are, so she must have had massive thighs! The others were quite slim!

One night in the eighties, me, Sue (my former partner) and Pete Slights went up to The Stone Trough pub at Kirkham Abbey in my estate car with the legs strapped to the roof rack. We had stuck Sue's yellow wellies on them and she was leaning on these legs in the pub! On the way home, one of them flew off the roof rack, but we were that pissed we daren't stop to pick the bugger up! The next day there was a story in the local press saying they were looking for a one legged bloke who had lost a leg and a welly!!!

It wasn't in the Press really but I tell everyone that! It is such a good story! I still have the other leg in the workshop now!

2 – Yukspeed Window Cleaners

So, going back to my early days, I joined my dad in York and was window cleaning for a living. Yukspeed Window Cleaning or sometimes Yukspeed Glass Wall Maintenance Engineers International, as I called it. But before then I had done all sorts. When I was a kid, I used to help out at a local farm. I was just eight years old and driving anything I could lay my hands on: tractors, lorries, anything. I loved it. Pete Harrison was a local farmer at Upper Helmsley and I used to help out there, just so I could drive the tractors. They had an old converted bus made in to a flat back wagon.

I was only little, but I could reach the pedals and do the gears and when we were harvesting, I would drive this wagon. "Hold on tight!" I had to shout otherwise I would get a bollocking from the bloke on top as he would tumble off! That is what started me becoming a petrol head.

At thirteen, I was delivering groceries, helping out at farms on weekends – anything to make money. I would always have a go at any job available. I was a butcher, I sold hot dogs

First taste of driving on the farm.

in York on a night then finally started my window cleaning business. It cost me £14 for a set of ladders and I have still got them, still use them! I bought them on finance and I'm still paying for them now!!

3

I had the window cleaning business for about three years. I had a good client base from when I was a butcher going round the villages in my butcher's van – all the villages round the north of York.

3 – Yukspeed Car Sales

Then I started dabbling in cars a little bit, buying and selling. That is when I first started rallying. My first car was a 1293 Cooper S. I did a few road rallies, me and Roger Butler. Well, he couldn't navigate and I couldn't drive! We ended up one night going down a river bed! It was plot and bash and Roger hadn't a clue what was going on. We got out of the river eventually but I don't know how!!!

Then another night event, he slots me into this farm track which takes us into a farm yard and there were all these bales in the way. We gets out and starts moving these bales out of the way. Where did we end up? In the middle of a field! We had to shove the bales back again to get back out!! I didn't know he was that crap at navigating!

First rally we ever did, we started at car 127. Being a bit green about rallying, I thought I had to pass the whole lot of them to win!!!

Another time I took Pip Dale (a quick, local driver) with me. He was wearing his farm overalls and a pair of wellies! We did various airfields around North Yorkshire. On Tholthorpe Airfield, we went straight on into a shit heap and Daley had to get out and push! He says to me, "That's why I'm wearing 'me wellies!" We then went off into the night to do the night road sections. Anyway, we were near Hawnby on the Yorkshire Moors. We came whizzing down this hill, took off sideways and hit the nose of the Mini into this bridge! We had to go back and repair the bridge with sand and mortar the next day.

The halfway halt was at Kirkbymoorside and we met Gig North, who offered Pip some spare spotlights. Pip said, "Get lost, we don't want those. He's tried to kill us sixteen times already! Let's go 'ome." But I wasn't having any, I wanted to carry on.

We set off again and headed over this bloody moor near Bransdale to the next selective. As I went to put it into second gear, it wouldn't come out of first. We had to go all the way in bottom gear. Somehow we managed to eventually finish the event. I was desperate to get a finish and another signature on my licence. In those days you had to get six signatures to go stage rallying. All I wanted to do was forest rallying, really, 'cos I can't see in the dark, never have been able to!

So, by now, I hadn't got a clutch and someone was towing me. The engine was smoking and boiling. We stopped at the side of the road and I took the bloody drive shaft out so we could tow it and get the daft thing home.

We finally got it home to my dad's house in York. I rang my girlfriend and I told her I would be there at 5 o'clock that night. Well, I slept all the way through and missed her!

By this time, around 1972, I was working with Bill Lumb at Escrick Service Station. I was still window cleaning, but winding that business down 'cos cars were taking over. Then I finally got into stage rallying at last! I had enough signatures to upgrade. Bill was rallying Piggy Thompson's old Mk. I Escort, with a Volvo engine in it because, by now, Piggy had the lovely green BDA Escort that Tony Drummond built him; CVN 950L.

So, I decided to transfer the Yukspeed name from window cleaning to car sales, specialising in Minis. I used to deal in Minis all the time. You'd buy a trade-in from a BMC dealer; you'd have to change the sub-frames, steering rack, brake pipes, new sills on them and repaint them. All that fuckin' work for £295! Mind you, that was a load of money in those days. You could have a full night out for £1 in those days: packet of fags, packet of Durex, a pork pie and half a cider!

I bought this Mini in 1969 which I couldn't sell, so I broke it and the bits started to sell quite well. Bill was dabbling in Twin Cam Escorts, and I was dealing in Mini stuff. There was an old bloke called Judd Midgley at Stockton-on-Forest, just outside York. He'd ring me up and say, "Now Yuk, I've been offered one of them their Cooooooper things. Will tha' come with me and buy it and give me a drink out of it?" He had a Morris Oxford with a trailer made from a caravan chassis, a two wheeler thing. We would go up to The Wolds somewhere and buy this Mini Cooper. We used to pick it up with the car on the trailer; it used to wag all over the road at 35-40 mph!

Of course, we would have to call at all the pubs on the way back! He'd say, "Well, I'll just 'ave 'alf a bitter... and put a double vodka in the top." We had to go on a detour off the main road to visit all the pubs in the villages, like! He never took any money off us.

More stock arrives at Escrick

I couldn't afford to do a lot of rallies but I enjoyed servicing for a few people. You learn a lot doing that. I did The Scottish Rally once for a young buck called John Coulter (an art dealer from York who would buy and sell fine art). He used to race Formula 5000 as well as rally. John rallied a Hillman Imp Californian then went down to Coventry and bought a proper works Imp: JDU 48E.

Well, he came into service in the Imp this one time with the car stuck in 3rd gear. We ran out of time trying to fix it and he went OTL (over time limit). We dropped the sump guard and this little pebble dropped out! It had jammed the linkage where it went into the gearbox!

Me and Lubo (Bill Lumb) did a bit of servicing for him and looked after the race and rally cars sometimes. I learnt a lot from Bill too.

Jonny Coulter, Mike Reynard and Billy Wood all ran these Formula 5000 race cars. We went all over the UK doing races with these cars. We were up at Croft and the bar was on the infield where the chicane still is today. Outside the bar was a big bed of roses, and Jonny had bought one of those monkey bikes for races and rallies. We decided that to determine whose round it was, we would have races around this rose bed on the monkey bike and whoever was slowest on three laps bought the round! We would all be pissed up! Well, I thought I can't be last 'cos I haven't got any fuckin money! We used to make sure Jonny or Billy was slowest 'cos they had plenty of money did those lads!!

Anyway, as we got more and more pissed the challenges got tougher! Jonny challenged the Vauxhall saloon car racing driver Gerry Marshall to a race from one end of the grid to the other for £20... on foot! Now Gerry was a big lad and I mean big! Anyway, Gerry won!!

It got worse when it was suggested that Lubo couldn't get around the circuit in less than two minutes in an old HA Viva van with all tools and wheels chucked in back! So me and Bill jumped into this little Vauxhall Viva van and we set off round the circuit in this fully loaded up van! We hurtled along the old Railway Straight and then around the back of the circuit, but the old van kept going wide and Bill was having all on to keep her on the road as all the stuff in the back would slide around and we just couldn't get it under the two minutes!

I says, "let's slow down, take the tool box out and that should do it." Bill pulls up at the side of the circuit and we chucks all the stuff out onto the grass and sets off again. There no seat belts in those days, like! Well, we had to get under two minutes 'cos there was a fiver bet on and neither of us had any money!!!! We would get locked up these days, wouldn't we?!

I serviced for Bilko too (one-armed Mike Jackson) and Steve Howard and the Crystals Rally Team from Hull, including an RAC which started from York. Then Piggy came on the scene so I ended up looking after him (Bilk wasn't very amused! "You were quite happy servicing for me until bloody Piggy comes along!"). Then I started doing a few more events myself.

The results were starting to come a bit on local stage events and I was getting better seedings, but I had never run first on the road. In 1975, still in a Mini, we did a local event called the Moore's Opel Stages Rally which was mainly farm tracks, stubble fields and airfields. It was sponsored by the local Opel dealers at that time. Some good lads were doing it like Colin "Mad Dan" Grewer in his Gp. 1 Opel Ascona and other quick local folk in big Gp. 4 Escorts like Dick Rowland, but leading and eventual winner was Tony Fall testing in a works Gp. 2 Opel Ascona. We were somewhere in the top ten at the time and we had a hold up for whatever reason. I says, "Can I go first on the road, please lads?"

Tony Fall says, "yeah, course you can!"

So there is me in my little old cobbled together Mini, first on the road on this stage in front of a works Ascona and all the top local lads in their big Escorts! It was like a highlight of my life was that!

One rally I was doing in the Mini in Lincolnshire with Alf Smith, at the stage arrival, Rob Pilcher was stood talking to Alf. Next thing, Alf jumps out and Rob sits in, so he did a stage with me!!!

Another time, me and Daley had entered the Scarborough Stages, I think it was (Mike Nicholson talks about this in his book) and my race engine in the Mini dropped a valve a couple of days before the event. I had a look around the shed and I found a bog standard 850cc engine which I had lying about and dropped that in!

Well the bloody thing would hardly move but once we got to Oliver's Mount at Scarborough, we were having such a good time! We were supposed to come in after two laps, but Daley says, "Come on let's do another!"... then another... then another.

We loved it, so we just kept going till we ran out of fuel! The fuckin' stage commander was jumping up and down! By, we did laugh!

Bill Lumb

4 – Willy, I'm going to die!

It would be the late sixties, early seventies when I first met Yuk. I was navigating on a rally with Jonny Coulter in his Hillman Californian (fast back shaped Hillman Imp version). It was a local road rally, York Motor Club's Spring Rally, I think.

We started in York and from the start, we had to drive out of town towards the first time control which was up near Castle Howard (funnily enough not far from where Yuk now lives!), to start the competitive bit. We were expected to trundle our way out of the city and up on to the A64 at a very low average speed then to re- group before the first competitive section. To our amusement, this Mini comes screaming past us all, overtaking all the competitors and heading up the road at quite a speed, even though he was seeded about ten places behind us!

We arrived at the first control and this Mini was parked up, so once we had got back into position, I wandered over to have a word and explained he didn't need to go so fast on that section! It turned out it was his first rally and he had no idea about anything! We got on well from that first moment on!

We ended up doing a lot of events together, often servicing on rallies together for others and then we ended up sharing my service station at Escrick just outside York. I remember him coming down one day and he said, "Can I just put my car in your workshop to do a certain job?"

"Yes, of course you can," I replied and eight years later he was still there!

We never had any formal arrangements, but he would help out when I needed him and he would have his own corner of the workshop and keep bits and pieces under the bench. Then, of course, there was always the 'Gorilla Shed' too! This shed housed various spare tyres and parts. It got its name because in those days there were lots of free calendars around in the motor trade from various manufacturers. One particular calendar had this naked girl sat astride a tyre; her private parts resembled a hairy gorilla!

One day I heard shouting coming from the shed so I stopped what I was doing and ran out of the workshop around the corner and looked through the door of the shed. Yuk had fallen off a stack of tyres and was lying spread-eagled on the floor. He said, "Willy, I've had it, I've had it! I'm going to die!

I said, "No, hang on I'll give the doctors a ring!"

He said, "I don't think I will last that long!"

So I said, "Well what can I do then?"

And he says, "Just leave me here, I'll be alright. If I die, you can have my rally car!"

I couldn't leave him like that, so I took him down to the doctors and he got over it!

Starting up my business meant I didn't do many rallies myself in the early years of setting it all up but we had a fair few adventures. In the mid 1970s, the RAC Rally started from York. The Fiat works team got in touch and hired me and Yuk to look after one of the Fiat 131s and a team of mechanics in their vans on the rally. None of them could speak a word of English and they needed someone to negotiate with the owners of forecourts to be shut so we could service there. They gave me a bag of money to help the process along! Yuk and I did that together. It was quite an experience working with such star names as Markku Alen, Timo Salonen and so on.

At the finish of the RAC, we were gathered around in the headquarters and all the usual PR/marketing was going on for various things including a new rally we had never heard of called The Donegal Rally. There was a promotional film from the previous year which Yuk and I watched and we looked at each other and said, we have to do this!

We bought a cracking good Mini engine and gearbox off Keith Stones; it came out of his rallycross car. It had an 8 port head and we built up this Mini to do the event in. Well, what a great event it was and we were leading the class at the time, but for some reason, suddenly the tie rod disappeared out of the front of the suspension and made the car a pig to drive, especially with a limited slip diff. The car was undriveable and sadly we had to retire.

So Yuk then bought his ex-works World Cup Rally Mk. 1 Twin Cam rolling shell from Guy Lockwood. When we were building it up, we found all sorts of interesting bits and pieces in the shell including a special tray which was built into the foot-well by the passenger door under the trip meter. It contained a bloody great machete for the World Cup Rally adventures!

Anyway, we used this car for the following year's Donegal. We couldn't afford an intercom so we made one up using a bit of piping and a funnel. I would talk through the funnel and the other end of the tube went into Yuk's helmet! It worked a treat!

We had some giddy evenings acting daft after having a few beers. One night we ended up having the usual water fight in the hotel. I would knock on people's bedroom doors and as they answered them, Yuk would chuck water all over them! One of these nights, Phil Short (co-driving for the semi works driver, John Taylor) got soaked and he was not amused! He definitely had a sense of humour failure that night! That was another fine mess Yuk got me into!

As a thank you for this big party of visitors from the UK, the hotel manager had given Yuk two bottles of poteen (pronounced 'pocheen' – a very potent, illegal, traditional Irish form of moonshine). We all set off for home in a big convoy. I was driving the Escort with my son in with me. We had only got three or four miles outside Letterkenny when we all stopped. Yuk runs back to see me and says, "Willy, we have forgotten the poteen!"

As it had been a gift from the hotel manager to all of us, I turned around and headed back for the poteen in the rally car. Meanwhile, the convoy continued ahead confident we would catch them up.

As we headed back to join the convoy, we were going like stink. When we came over a hill at the other side, the Irish army had a road block set up! Of course, we had two bottles of illegal poteen rolling around on the floor of the rally car as we got pulled up at the check point!

Fortunately, they said, "Oh, you are one of the rally lads – give us a wheelie!" and let us go! Phew, we got away with it!

We had an after rally party at our house when we finally got home and Tony Coward tells a good story about the results of that!

Yuk had various girlfriends over the years. I met most of them at some time or other.

The only thing in life that Yuk is interested in is rallying... and women... and booze!... and wheeling and dealing... or is it women first... selling bits second... rallying third and then booze fourth! Or is it, booze first...

5 – Yuk finds a gun!

I went servicing for Jonny Coulter on the Firestone Rally in Spain in 1969. He had his beautiful ex-works Imp (JDU) I mentioned earlier. We had to have temporary import papers for all the spares, the service barge and the race car. It was all in triplicate and you had to show them to people when you went into Spain and leave them a copy. When you left Spain, you got a copy back and had to check you had got all the bits; it was called a 'carni eia', a temporary import paper.

Me and this lad called Gig North (I mentioned him earlier) were servicing and Chris Gray from Scarborough was navigating for Jonny. Well, I couldn't navigate for toffee, I hadn't a clue. Gig was driving this Hillman Hunter estate car – we had a spare engine in the back as well; we were a bit posh, we were!!

Somehow with me navigating we ended up in France! We were heading for the border... 'cos the rally was based at the Firestone factory near Santander in Northern Spain where you came in off the ferry. Somehow we ended up at this border control and this bloke says, "Papers, papers!" I just gave this bloke a folder full of papers and he gives us the folder back; so we sets off and I says to Gig, "Gig, we're in France, I don't think we should be! We should be in Spain!"

We turns round and this fuckin' bloke just waves us through. Unbeknown to me, he had kept the carni eia!!

Anyway, we get the rally over with. It had been quite a long old rally which was an overnight and day job. At the finish, we got pissed of course and we were so tired we were falling asleep in our soup at the dinner table; it was horrendous!

We gets up the next day to get to our ferry and Jonny says, "Where are all the papers, passports and carni eia?"

"Haven't got a clue," says I.

"Well, we can't leave the country without it; we will have to take the race car home and leave the barge and spares here!"

I says, "Ahh, we'll sort it out Jonny. The only place we could have lost it will be the French border."

Jonny says, "Well what the fuck were you doing at the French border?!"

I says, "My navigating skills were getting tested there, John!"

So we gets to the ferry. They would let the race car go, let all us four get on the boat but the barge had to stay here 'cos we hadn't got the papers. We pleaded with them: "You know we had all bits when we arrived and we still have all the bits now; you must let us through." But oh no, they weren't having any of it.

So what do we do now? We decided Gig and Chris would take the rally car back, then there is me and John stuck in Spain not being able to speak a fuckin' word of Spanish with the barge. "British Consulate, that's where we need to be. We'll go there!" says Jonny.

We gets there and this Yorkshire bloke was the boss. We goes in. "Now then, lads," he says in a proper Yorkshire accent! We were nearly in tears to find someone who could speak not only English but good old Yorkshire an' all!

We explained the situation: that the papers we needed might have been left at the border control at the Spanish/French border. "Aye" he says, "well don't worry, they owe me a favour. I could ring them now and they are probably on their desk, but they are so laid back. Leave it with me and contact me in the morning."

"Oh thank you so much," we says.

So we gets back to the barge. Now to this day, I don't know why we had a fuckin' gun in a rag box in the back of the fuckin' Hunter! It was a pistol, a bit like a starting pistol!

"Jonny, what the fuck are we doing with a fuckin' gun?!!!!" Now don't forget this was the time that there was lots of unrest; General Franco and all that – don't say this, don't say that. There is us, in trouble with a fuckin' gun in the car; no fuckin' race car but we've got a gun!

So next day, we contact our friend at the Consulate and he says, "Right lads, get your ferry booked this evening. We have got your carni eia coming back now."

We gets the barge back down to the docks in plenty of time. We wanted to be the first in the fuckin' queue to get back home. We couldn't wait to leave all this behind.

I says, "John, we've got to get rid of this fuckin gun. If they find it, we'll be in jail and they'll chuck keys away!!!!"

It was a red hot day in Spain, of course, and we were walking along the jetties, where the docks are, with our rally jackets on, sweating in all this heat, with a fuckin' gun under the jacket!

Of course, John gives the fuckin' gun to bloody muggins, "Here, you carry it, Yuk."

I says, "What are we going to do with it?"

He says, "Chuck it in harbour!"

We must have looked like some dodgy looking characters! I chucks the fuckin' thing into the harbour.

We go back to the Consulate and the form has arrived! We are hugging him and kissing him! We finally gets on the ferry and we takes this bastard of a customs officer for a drink! Well, we were pissed up in no time at all! We were just so relieved to get on and to be heading back home!!

Sailing home, the sea gets rougher and rougher and the boat is rocking about all over the place, so much so, we fell off our stools at the bar! When we finally got to bed it was so rough we couldn't keep anything down!!

Apparently it was the roughest sea crossing they had that year. By, we were so glad to be back home, but what an experience!

We were English lads abroad without a clue! Still don't know to this day why that gun was there.

6 – Yuk gets introduced to malt whisky!

It would be 1968/69 time, servicing for Jonny Coulter on one of the classic Scottish rallies up at Grantown on Spey. It was great rallying up in Scotland. Everyone was so friendly and welcoming. It was the first time we had been to Scotland and we thought it was great; 'haggis and Och ey the noo' and all that! We got into this hotel, there was quite a gang of us there; the late Colin "Mad Dan" Grewer, Jonny Coulter and Phil Welch... who was stood on a table reciting Eskimo Nell until he proceeded to fall off it! We met Hamish Hanna who introduced me to the top shelf stuff, "Aye Yuk you have got to drink whisky when you are in Scotland," he said in his broad Scottish accent!

It was Dan who had to carry me upstairs to my bedroom after.

By, was I sick!!!

7 – My YUC 405 number plate

We used to go to the car auctions in Scarborough, me and Lubo. We would buy all sorts of fuckin' things; never made any money like!!

I saw it on a 1956 Ford Consul – YUC 405 – £17 tax and tested. So we drove it home, went down to the tax office in Petergate in York and filled the forms in, took the number plate off and it cost me a fiver to do it!

That plate went on a few Minis and then on to my Escorts too.

Wish I hadn't sold it though!

> **So, how did you get the name Yuk?**
>
> Fucked if I know!

Martin Welch

8 - The pile cream incident

The pile cream incident was on a Scottish Rally in the early seventies when we were servicing for Piggy. We were heading up to Scotland in Piggy's van. Piggy was driving the service van. I was sat at the other side and we had Fatty Jeff (who was a pipe smoker) with us sat in the middle seat in the front. Yuk was in the back with all the spares and bits and pieces.

We were just getting through Newcastle when Yuk asked us to stop outside a chemist shop because he was having trouble with his piles and he didn't have any treatment cream with him! So we pulled up at the side of the road and Fatty Jeff decides to go in too.

Yuk comes back, climbs into the back, drops his trousers then realises he had not bought an applicator! He looks around for something to apply the cream with; well there is Fatty Jeff's pipe resting on the dashboard! He gets a good old spoonful of cream in the pipe end and you know where it all goes! "Don't say anything to Fatty Jeff!" says Yuk. Jeff returns and we set off once again down the road.

The journey is settling down now and Fatty Jeff is relaxing and decides he wants to light his pipe. He gets his pipe stoked up with tobacco ready to light and he is just about to put it in his mouth when Yuk says, "Oh, Fatty Jeff, I wouldn't put that in your mouth I have just used it to apply my pile cream!"

Poor old Fatty Jeff went bananas! By, we did laugh!

There were so many incidents over the years. There was the time when Yuk and Wriggy (Alan Wrigglesworth) were sleeping in the van on one event. In the middle of the night Yuk woke up needing a pee. There was a large plastic water bottle in the back and thought, "Well it's only used for the radiator of the car or washing the rally car down," so he peed in to that rather than getting out in the middle of a cold night.

Next morning, Wriggy decides he needs to freshen up a bit and... well you guessed it, poured some water out into a bowl and splashed his face in it! So that caused a few problems!

Most Mondays we would to meet up at a really nice pub in Warthill just outside York which specialised in really nice steaks. We would have our steaks, discuss the adventures of the last rally that weekend, for instance, and plan what we were going to do next.

This particular night, Yuk meets this girl and takes her off to a cottage not far from the pub. Me and a couple of other guys decides to go and see where they had gone. We found a ladder and we all climbed up it to find Yuk in bed with this girl in the upstairs bedroom of the cottage. She is sat on top with her back to the window.

Yuk sees us three peering through the window and puts the bedside light on, gives us a wink and gets back to it! Then the ladder started to slip and we all had to exit sharpish!

Piggy's CVN receives service

First time I met Yuk was at an autotest in the late sixties at Melbourne airfield. There were lots of smart Mini Cooper S's and Ford Lotus Cortinas (the cars of the day) and Yuk turns up in his tired old, lime green Mini van which he used to window clean with (Yukspeed Window Cleaners). He took the back doors off so he could see where he was reversing! But he acquitted himself very well.

I remember Yuk telling us about a mansion house he used to go to clean windows at and he was on top of the ladder one day, quite high up and he felt the ladders slipping away so he grabbed hold of the guttering which gradually peeled away and he came down to the ground! He decided not to charge them but made a run for it and never went back again!

Yuk was an excellent service crew member. He worked quickly and didn't mind getting dirty. He was resourceful and, of course, always such good company! By 1973, Piggy and I were doing the national rally championship and Yuk would service for us on nearly every round. The commitment and money by this stage was getting serious so I decided *to retire from rallying altogether. Piggy was doing very, very well and lots of talented and ambitious co-drivers were ready to step into my shoes. People like Mike Nicholson, Mike Greasley and Dave Richards soon took over and went with Piggy from strength to strength.*

Yuk, Piggy and Wriggy

Philip Welch
9 - Servicing with Yuk in the early days

I think it was about 1973 on the Scottish Rally. Martin, my brother, would be co driving for Colin "Mad Dan" Grewer and I was navigating the service barge. I had Yuk with me in the van helping me service for Dan. We hired the van from a rental company in York. We also hired an Austin Cambridge estate car as a chase car. The estate car was driven by Pip Dale and the car was so overloaded with spares and bits and pieces that it struggled to stay on the road... it would sway about, go sideways around bends; it was here, there and everywhere. You wouldn't believe it!

When they took the vehicles back to the rental company, they were half cleaned up but left around the corner because they were in such a state... when the rally stickers were taken off the van, a load of paint came off too!

Super Mick (Mick Penrose)
10 - Yuk is crazy – how right I was!

I met Yuk in 1973. I was working down the road at another garage and passed Escrick Service Station going home to Riccal, just outside York. Bill Lumb had asked me if I fancied servicing for him on the Jim Clark Rally after he bought Piggy's Escort Mk. 1 with the Volvo engine fitted. On meeting Yuk, as an impressionable young guy, I thought Yuk was crazy.. and how right I was!

My introduction to rallying had me hooked and, as an apprentice mechanic, I would finish work at 5.00pm and go straight to Yuk's place and start helping him prepare his rally car until about 10.00pm. Then we would head down to the pub for a few jars! We pretty well did that every night of the week!

Yuk would sell his Minis on the front forecourt. He had a particularly nice one which he sold on to this chap, but only days later the chap came back to explain his son had borrowed it and rolled the thing! Yuk took the car back off him and we removed the roof, welded the doors shut and made her into an autotest car. "Come on Mick, let's see if you can drive her alright," said Yuk, and sent me down the forecourt, handbrake at the end and back up again.

"Yep," he said, " I think you are going to be fine," and I took up autotesting and did really well.

Next to the workshop was a store, a corrugated iron shed Yuk called the "Gorilla shed" which Bill mentions. Any unsuspecting lass who could be coerced into the shed was generally in for a shock and came out somewhat dishevelled!

11 - David and Goliath – Elcar Rally 1975

One of the best results we had in my big engined Mini (a really good 1380 cc motor) was the Elcar Rally in '75 with Pip Dale. Pip was a top driver himself and got lots of really good results on Motoring News events and, later on, stage events too in the Leedham's of York cars.

Anyway, Pip was navigating for me on this one. The Elcar Rally was a classic clubman event in its day. Organised by Huddersfield Motor Club, it was a 190 mile route with 50 miles of stages comprising mainly of old war time airfields and farm tracks scattered around the local area. It would easily fill its available 120 entries.

Lubo (Bill Lumb) was down to navigate when the entry went in, but then he buys a Mk. 2 Cortina and decides to do the rally himself. Pip Dale says he will do it with me. His wife wasn't too happy though, remembering what happened last time we rallied together!

George Beever was favourite to win as he had a beautiful works spec Clarke and Simpson/ David Sutton BDA Mk. I Escort. He was a good local driver with plenty of wins under his belt and a good team behind him.

Yuk and Pip Dale at scrutineering

We did the first stage, a farm track called Wighill. Poor old John Cockerill 's car seizes up on the start line, so that was one less Escort to worry about! I had fitted an LSD (limited slip differential) to the Mini for the first time and didn't know what the car was going to do as it was all twitchy on the road, but once on the loose it became very controllable. Result: 5 seconds behind George Beever who definitely had the best car for the event.

Then we did a couple of old aerodromes like Tockwith and Elvington. Well, Elvington had a two and half mile straight (no chicanes in those days to slow you down!). This was useless for my little Mini doing six and half thousand revs flat out in top and misfiring like hell! We lost about three weeks to Beever there! We changed the plugs and went on to knobbly tyres for Allerthorpe, which was dead rough but a right good thrash! Poor old George Beever goes off for two and half minutes. Never mind!

Melbourne airfield was next. After completing 2 laps, we were 26 seconds behind Beevers. Stage 6 was Churchill. Daley says he knows this one and could he drive? I said – yes, if I can go and stand at the finish! He must think I'm stupid! The stage was bumpy and we were jumping all over the road! We were 11 seconds behind.

Elcar Rally 1975, Yuk's first big result.

Full Sutton Airfield was next. We did the stage, got to the finish and a youth in a Porsche asked what our time was. It turned out we equalled his time! He wouldn't believe it.

Burton Fields next, half loose, half tarmac; we are 3 seconds behind Beevers.

Back to Elvington now to start the last six stages again. Nothing went wrong until Burton Fields, a farm track which Daley knew quite well. He was good, shouting at me which lines to take and he says, "Don't fuckin' lift until you get over the crest."

Well, we flew through the air! There were these 5 gallon drums just over the crest and they were pinging off the sides as we hit 'em! We missed a plough at the side of the road by about 18 inches!!! We were 1 second up there.

We finished up at the finish at Stamford Bridge which was at The Three Cups Inn and Poncho (Pete McNeil) asks, "How have you got on?"

"I haven't got a clue, Pete."

"Oh, you were second at halfway."

"Don't be ridiculous!" It was only a 1380 Mini with split Webbers but sure enough, we were second overall – only 20 seconds in it from George Beever in a works spec Escort! It was a real David and Goliath moment!

By, fuckin' 'ell... Leyland's gonna ring me up and offer me a drive! It was a good result; we did get pissed!

That was my first big result and I thought, now I need to be movin' into this Ford stuff.

12 - There's a goat in the kitchen!

We did the Donegal one year in a Mini I borrowed off Vince Chapman.

We broke a rear stud. They are only a 3/16 UNF stud. One of the local Irish lads says, "I know a bloke who has a couple of old works Minis in his shed."

So off we set in my car – we had a few beers before we set off. We gets out to the middle of nowhere and comes across a little farmstead with some Nissan huts and barns outside. The old boy was there. "Ahhh, come in lads, come in and have a drink! Do you want a drop of whisky?"

"Aye," I says. "Is it Scotch or Irish?"

"Well, living in Ireland, it is Irish whisky!"

So he gets the bottle out and we sit down... then there is a great crash and a bang outside and there is this goat jumping up at the kitchen window!

"Mary get the fuckin' goat in before he breaks the fuckin' window!"

So this goat comes in and we are drinking this 'ere whisky and the goat jumps up onto the draining board and starts braying at the window again!

First ever Donegal

"Mary, get the fuckin' goat out before it breaks the fuckin' window!"

We couldn't believe this carry on and we still hadn't seen any Minis yet! Finally we gets outside and he opens this barn door up and there are a couple of these works coloured Minis and a big box full of spares! He had a box full of wheel studs. "Here," he says, " take half a dozen of them!"

"How much do you want?"

"Fuck all!" he says, so I gave him a fiver. We fitted them the next morning and away we went; sorted!

Typical Ireland that.

13 – Yuk goes Ford

So, determined to go Ford and to start getting some serious results, I went to see the bank manager and I gets a £1000 overdraft which was lots of money then! I had to take my auntie as a guarantor!

Then I goes to see Guy Lockwood, who had this supposedly ex-works Roger Clark World Cup spec Escort. It was a complete car, less engine and box for £500. Pip Dale had owned her and then Guy. They both had good results with the car, so I wrote out a cheque for £500.

Yuk's first Escort

Now I needed an engine. Rob Pilcher and Jim Clark from York had been sharing an ex-Sunderstrom, ex-works Cortina, but they fell out over a bird so they were selling up. Jim had kept the engine, Rob kept the rolling chassis. So I went up to Jim's and there was the engine under the bench complete with Webbers and manifold ready to line up to my gearbox....£130! It was a lot of money, though. So for £630, I had an Escort Twin Cam. Just the job!

I think it was Bass Charrington – the first rally I did in '75 or '76, and I don't know where we finished. It had a Jag axle with drum brakes on and a standard Cortina gearbox in. I also got my first bit of sponsorship as well, from Ziebart rust proofing. I don't know how that came about, but they insisted the car was white with Ziebart blue lettering and my old service barge, a 1600 Crossflow Cortina estate, had to be in the exact same colours.

I managed to get some press coverage for the deal but put my foot in it when I said to the Press man, "I don't know why Ziebart are bothering; rally cars are usually crashed before they rot!"

We got some reasonable results with that car though, including 9th overall on the Lakeland and 17th on Donegal International Rally. We did loads of rallies in that car, even an RAC in 1976 with Eddie Ganderton.

We were starting to get in amongst the top lads now, even though most of them were now moving on to BDAs. We were doing a local event in the Twin Cam on an airfield event and Steve Howard who was co-driving for Bilko (one armed Mike Jackson) in the Crystals Escort came up to me and says, "Oh, Bilko has broken his arm!!!"

"Fuckin' 'ell!" I says.

So I walked up to Bilko's car to see if he was alright, worried for him 'cos he only has the one arm and he would be knackered without it, only to find Bilko sat in the rally car with a Phillips screw driver screwing the fingers back onto his false hand!!!! It was wooden in them days with a glove on it!!! It wasn't his good hand but his false one!! His fingers on his false hand had got stuck in the spokes of the steering wheel and he got crossed up and broke them!!!

What a hero!!!

14 – The French man and his little onions

In the 1970s, when I was still based in Escrick at Bill's place, me and some of the lads including Mick Penrose were in Ziggy's Night Club, or as it was then 'The 71 Club'. Outside was this nice little Renault Alpine. We got talking to this French lad who owned it, so he came up to see us the next day at the garage to show off his car.

He took me for a ride up the road in it and, fuckin' hell, it flew! With it being a little plastic racing car, it went like fuck round the corners. I was shitting myself! I could hardly go that speed in my Escort!

We gets back to the garage and I says, "right, you come with me in my Escort Twin Cam."

Ohhhhh! I had him holding on to his little onions!!!

John Forrest
15 – The Trannie incident!!!

I was doing an Airedale and Pennine Motor Club organised rally with Colin "Mad Dan" Grewer in 1975. The rally started from Ilkley and was based at the Craiglands Hotel; it may have been the Menston Stages. After successfully completing scrutineering, we all gathered at the hotel and we notice Yuk has had a skinful and he meets this gorgeous looking girl with well-manicured nails and perfect make up.

Not much later, Yuk orders a bottle of champagne and disappears up to his room with this girl and the bottle of shampoo! The landlord and all the locals glance at each other with knowing looks...

Ten minutes later Yuk comes back down looking absolutely crestfallen... it was only a well-known transvestite he had fallen for!

Super Mick (Mick Penrose)
16 – Crest Hotel mayhem!

Staying away on rallies usually meant getting soaking wet at some point! One night, staying in Grimsby at the Crest Hotel, I managed to find my bedroom after an absolute skin full! I had just got undressed when there was a knock on my bedroom window! I was three floors up!

Next minute, there was a knocking on my door and shouting... as I opened it, Lubo (Bill Lumb) chucked this bucket full of cold water over me! Me and the bedroom got a soaking! Of course I had to get him back, so even though I was completely naked, I filled my waste paper bin full of water, knocked on the bedroom door next to mine and as Lubo opened his door, I tried drenching him back!

It seemed then a great idea for both of us to go and find Yuk's room and give him similar treatment! We were both bollock naked, but filled our bins full of water and giggling went to the lift and pressed the button. Yuk's room was on the first floor. It was a surreal moment when the two of us got in to the lift – giggling and laughing and naked – but we both stopped and remained silent in the lift whilst we went down two floors... one of those strange moments where you just don't talk to people in lifts, do you? That would be just weird!!!

17 – Yuk co-drives for Piggy

First time co-driving was for Piggy in his first rally Porsche 911. It was the Lindisfarne Rally up on the Scottish Borders in 1975.

Although he was very quick driver and very enthusiastic... and had all the right equipment, he wasn't that organised, wasn't Piggy. It was all a bit last minute and suddenly he realised he hadn't got a co-driver so he says, "Right, come on, Yuk, me and you can do it!"

Well, I was shitting myself, not a clue what I was doing. Fortunately in those days, it wasn't pace notes, so I didn't have to worry about that! It was just maps and the road book to sort out, but I was crap. If it had been me, I would have sacked myself!

So, we gets through a few stages, then on the eighth stage we visited the scenery after the brake lines kept busting and Piggy was running out of brakes. Luckily, in the end, Piggy got fed up and we retired! I was so relieved!

I always used to buy Motoring News and Autosport and Peter Newton wrote in Autosport in the 9th October 1975 edition,

"Piggy Thompson brought along the Page Animal Feeds Porsche and inside beaming ear to ear the infamous 'Yuk', sometime Mini pilot and ebullient post rally party exponent. The pair had already passed a highly satisfactory pre rally evening."

I says to Bill, "Ebullient...ebullient! What's that mean?" Bill says "it means you're a pervert!"

Anyway, co driving was not really for me, but then years later, I end up doing it again for Piggy in his Starion Turbo in the '80s!

I have always been useless with maps. Once, I took Jonny Coulter down south to an airport somewhere (!) and thought I would go and see my mam who was living in Bristol by that time. I hadn't seen her for quite a few years so thought I would visit her on my way back up North.

I was in a Range Rover (which had just come out) and headed up the M4 to Bristol. I left the next day to trundle up North then like a silly sod, I realised I forgotten my map! I turned off somewhere and stopped at this little village and asked someone where I was. I was only in the Lake District! This was over 50 miles North of where I should have been. It cost me about a million pounds in fuel to finally get to my home in York. Those old Range Rovers were a bit heavy on fuel!

Report written by Yuk for the York Motor Club magazine 1976.

18 – Letter from Letterkenny

"We left Esclit (Escrick, York) 12.30pm Tuesday 15th June 1976, destination Donegal. We arrived in Letterkenny at midnight, after passing through Londonderry checkpoints with army rifles popping through the windows. I was more than glad to get there!

On the boat going over, we met an Irish youth called John Connor, who was coming back from Glasgow. He had bought a 2 litre BDA to do his first rally in! Upon asking if it had a 5-speed ZF and discs on the rear, he promptly replies, 'yes'... has a think for ten seconds and burst out with, 'Fuckin' hell, I'm not sure, I never looked!"

Letterkenny

With no hotel booked, we must have knocked on twelve hotel/B+B doors before someone suggested Hannah Coughlan's, who made us very welcome. (Oh by the way, there was Lubo (Bill Lumb) and Super Smooth Mick (Mick Penrose), who were both sporting Flum Buff taches! Smelly [toe nail] Graham, young Anton also came along but don't ask for their proper names, I haven't a clue!

Wednesday 16th June

After acquiring a set of pace notes, we all jumped into the barge and went to check the notes against the road. I'm afraid we only managed four stages all day. The Smithwicks (local brew) sign kept calling us in, and with five of us in the car all disagreeing which was the best symbol for which particular bit of road, Lubo suggested it would be best if just him and I went out the next day!

Thursday 17th June

We checked six stages against the notes, then back for scrutineering. Everybody got through, including John with his 2 litre BDA. When asked by Kojak, the scrutineer, where his second brake master cylinder was, he pointed to the clutch cylinder and everybody was happy.

Friday 18th June – 11 stages

First car away was about 12.30pm. Me and Bill were seeded at 108 and started at 12.54 ... eh? After the first stage, we came in for service feeling happy but a little shaky. You couldn't help thinking about the possibility of a car coming the other way. Our borrowed intercom wasn't up to much. All I could hear was the Webbers sucking so after stage two, we threw it away. On the stage notes, everything is OK until the navigator gets lost. I seemed to go for miles with a bag of tatties in the hot seat (sorry Lubo). I know it is very difficult. Then suddenly he would start shouting again. Sometimes the instructions he gave me couldn't possibly have been in the notes! Anyway, on to stage ten.

When we came over the brow, the road went 90 right – we didn't – we went straight on into a bank! Lubo jumps out, pulled the wing off the tyre and away we went; only dropped 30 seconds.

There was one more stage before the overnight halt. We had no dramas until heading back when the water pump started rattling. The fan had broken and knackered the pump. Luck was on our side 'cos it never leaked for the rest of the event. We did 2 miles on the fourth stage on a flat tyre and had another between stages. This meant we were running 2 Kleber and 2 Goodyear on the car and they were on opposite corners! Looking at the results that night, we were 49th overall.

Saturday 19th June – 15 stages

It rained overnight. We had a good night on the Smiffwicks, so wasn't feeling too 'Derrick' the next day. We got caught by Bernard Banning on the 2nd stage, so thought I had better get my finger out and get the brain cleared. Lubo's voice was getting worse all the time.

We got motoring in the afternoon, but had to stop on a long stage to change a wheel. We also kept getting baulked so at night, what with brain fade, punctures and baulking, we had dropped 3 minutes to the class leader when we were 4 secs up on the first night. So it was bed early that night. This is getting serious. If we win the class, we're in for some lollipops.

Sunday 20th June – 13 stages

Next morning I felt ready for anything! I pysched the class leader and told him he'd got all his troubles to come. We took 20 seconds off him on the first stage,

10 seconds on next one, equal on the third, then he retired with a broken spring (hurray!). We had really got into the groove by now after having four good Dunlop Racers fitted. We had 8th and 10th fastest on two stages, which for a 1600 Twin Cam ain't bad going.

We got to the last stage and we are still going bananas, when half way through we crested a brow into immediate right and left. We both thought this is the big one! How we got away with it, Dunlop only knows! Back to the finish for all the fans and interviews. It felt as though I had won the Monaco Grand Prix. I've never seen such a big crowd. The whole of Ireland must have come to the rally.

Much Smiffwicks was consumed before, during and after the prize giving and the festivities went on until seven the next morning! We ended up 17th overall, 3rd Ford, 1st in Class, SFP class award and possibly a Kleber tyre award.

The Donegal is rated the best rally in the world. So much so, I've booked 30 beds for next year, so get your name down early. Oh, it was won by Brian Nelson in a Porsche Carrera.

Yours Smiffwickly,

Yuk"

It was such an exciting rally for us all – first time in a different country; closed roads, pace notes – no one ever went to bed, we all got pissed – if anyone did go to bed we would get the fire hose and stick it through their bedroom window and give them a blast!

Then we would get to a restaurant and everyone was throwing ice cubes; even the hotel manager was chucking ice cubes!! Mint!

Eddie Ganderton

19 – The '76 Lombard RAC Rally with Yuk

Yuk and I did quite a few small events together in his early rallying days in his Minis. We even did the famous Illuminations Rally in the Lake District, a very snowy Motoring News road event where we seemed to spend more time off the road than on, but he learnt quickly.

The biggest event for the two of us had to be the 1976 Lombard RAC Rally which started from Bath. We did it in his Mk. 1 Twin Cam Escort. This used to be a massive event, up to 180 entries some years, 5 days and 4 nights; it was really tough but we relished the challenge.

We got some backing from The Old World Club in Stonegate in York and I remember forking out a huge amount of money for the entry fee in those days, so it did not go down very well with me when we retired early on in Yorkshire in the dark! One minute we were flying, then we seemed to lose power, the lights went out and we ground to a halt. "Any ideas?" I said.

"It'll be the battery," says Yuk.

It was a second hand battery out of a Mini and it was knackered!

"You mean you spent about three quid on a second hand battery for an event like this?!" I said.

I was not impressed. That was Yuk all over though, he never had the budgets other people had, everything was on a shoestring.

Don't forget it was November, middle of the night in the Yorkshire forests and bloody cold and wet. I dug out my lovely warm sheepskin coat from the boot and went back down the track and found salvation in a well-heated caravan. Yuk turned up later just in his yellow sailor suit soaking wet, freezing and fed up! Mind you, this was Yuk; it didn't take long before he was laughing again!

Super Mick (Mick Penrose)
20 – Servicing on the '76 Lombard RAC Rally

Me and Jim Kilmartin were servicing for Yuk and Eddie in Yuk's knackered old Ford Cortina estate. The famous old Escort got through scrutineering then we discovered that the car had no brakes! We parked her up in a layby outside a Police station in Bath and fitted new brake cylinders!

It wasn't the best of starts. We were almost amazed the car got as far as Yorkshire before the battery let us down! There we were at the top of Sutton Bank in North Yorkshire in the dark, not much more than thirty minutes from home and we had to drive all the way back to Bath to get our bags and pick up the trailer! Yuk had a bit of spending money left and the hotel was paid for, so we drove back to Bath and stayed there for two days and got pissed!

21 – Yuk's first BDA

There I was trying to get results with my old Mk. I Twin Cam, but the trouble was everyone had moved up to 1700 BDAs, so I was always a step behind. So the year after, I built a Mk. 2 with help from Mucky Bob (Rob Nowell, a young mechanic from Stamford Bridge who was building up a fine reputation for building lovely Escorts in the York area) and a few others helped too.

I bought a 1700 BDA motor off John Laley for £1100. That took some saving up for. John was happy for me to take it before I had enough to pay for it but I insisted on paying him the whole amount before taking it away.

So I had just got going with that and the bastards had moved up to 2 litre BDAs so I was still behind them!! This Mk. 2 was a nice car, though. Mucky Bob, who helped build it – he was a clever lad. Tragically, he committed suicide some years later; don't know why. Lots of people helped build the car including Christine Coward's husband, Tony who did the wiring. He did a right mint job of that. Christine did a few events with me including my first event in the car, the Manx.

Super Mick (Mick Penrose) used to help and Jim Kilmartin (who now scrutineers on most local events) also used to help out. By this time, I had done a couple of events, but I ran out of money, so I sold the rolling chassis to Warren Philliskirk for about £1300. I had done a rally in Ireland with Ronan McManee in 1977 and a fucking core plug dropped out on one of the stages, so that was end of a lovely 1700 BDA!

Warren put his own engine in it and really started to get noticed in that car doing very well locally, winning lots of rallies and then going on to do BTDRA events too with Christine Parling.

Tony Coward
22 – Paid in peas!

Chris (Christine Coward) and I got to know Yuk over a period of time. Chris and I rallied together as a couple on road and stage events and we were generally seeded fairly close to Yuk and got to know him on events. I stopped competing but Chris wanted to carry on in the co-driver's seat, so she got rides with various drivers in the local area near Northallerton (in North Yorkshire) and I would help prepare the car and service on events.

Chris Coward

She got some top rides too with quick lads like Mike Taylor (of Mike Taylor Developments), Steve Smith (who later became famous for rallying Lancia Integrales and was also well known for his infamous crash on the Mintex Rally, going through the railings on the Marine Drive in Scarborough and landing in the sea!), Steve Shaw (in one of Yuk's old Mk. 2s YUC 405) and she went with many quick lady drivers of the time too, like the very determined Sandy Lawson who used to drive an ex-works DAF.

Anyway, Chris was keen to compete in the Huxford Ladies Rally Championship. Ladies registered for the championship and scored points, I think mainly, if not all, on Castrol Autosport Championship rounds. In 1977 Chris wanted to find a driver who would do a few rounds rather than just do local events, so rang a few people trying to find a regular ride in the championship. She rang Yuk and his instant reaction was, "Oh yeah, you can come with me," and we did one or two rounds but we also had to get rides with a couple of others as well to see the year through.

In 1978 Chris did the championship seriously (the last year of the Huxford Rally Championship) and won it! Once again, it had to be with several drivers as it was hard to find anyone who could commit to a full season. At the prize presentation at the end of the year, Chris won a huge trophy presented by Princess Anne and had afternoon tea with her!

One of the rallies with Yuk in 1977 was the Hadrian Centurion Rally which was based in Newcastle. Yuk and Chris did it in the white Ziebart sponsored Mk. 1 Twin Cam. We stayed at a small hotel in the city, which like most hotels, had a lift. We came back from having a meal out somewhere and went in to the reception area, pushed the button for the lift door to open, but it had labelled on it 'Restricted to 4 people'. We thought, "Oh, we'll all get in this alright", so all eight of us got in and off we went... for a little while... then it stopped! It wouldn't go up or down. The doors wouldn't open and we had all been drinking for several hours including Chris who drank pints too!

We pressed the bell and nothing happened (not too surprising as it was the early hours of the morning!) and we were all getting desperate for the loo! Eventually someone came and we had to shout upwards to this chap who said he would sort it out. It was taking forever for someone to come back to us and the pain of holding all this drink in was getting worse!

Finally, the doors got slowly prized open. It was the Newcastle Firemen with all the gear riving open the doors and then we had to wait for them to find some step ladders to lower down into the lift so we could get out! What the fire crew thought, I don't know because we all smoked in those days, they probably thought there was a fire too!

Anyway, Yuk and Chris did really well on the rally coming 9th overall in very good company as it was a Castrol/Autosport round. Paul Faulkner won in his Mk. 2 BDA and there were people like Nigel Rockey who was second and David Stokes third. All the other top lads in that period were there too, so it was a very competitive event and an excellent result.

When Yuk was building his very first Mk. 2, I would go down to his little workshop in Escrick on a weekend to help out a bit. One Saturday afternoon I arrived and he was looking a bit fed up. "What's up Yuk?" I asked.

"Ugh, I've not got much done this morning. A local farmer turned up at the workshop this morning in a panic. He says, "You've got to help me, you've got to help me; my harvester's broken down and I have got to get it going again quick!"

It was this man's pea harvester and they had to harvest the peas and get them in the freezer within hours. Local farmers in the area all had large contracts with companies such as Bird's Eye and Farrah's Peas and worked under tremendous time pressures.

Eventually, Yuk found the problem and sorted it for him and off he went. This bloke had given Yuk bags and bags and bags full of peas! Yuk never saw any money but plenty of peas!

Christine Coward
23 – The gold lamé suits!

Yuk and I decided to do the International Manx in 1977 in his new Mk. 2 Escort and we were making our plans for the event. Mucky Bob (Bob Nowell RIP) was to service for us as usual along with my husband Tony. Mucky Bob pointed out that Yuk always wore garish overalls when competing (yellow ones at that particular time!) and he said he thought we should all wear something garish too. That got me thinking.

Tony Coward modelling!

I used to do a bit of dress making at the time, so I took Tony and Bob down to the shops and they selected this awful gold lamé material which had clearly been in the shop for a long time as it was still priced in pounds, shillings and pence! I think the shop just let me have it in the end for nothing!

Yuk knew nothing of this little caper until the drivers' briefing at the rally on this sunny day, when I turned up to the meeting in my suit and stood next to him; he was gob smacked! Of course in those days, you didn't have to wear Nomex so I got away with it. "What the fuckin' hell... ?!!!" was his reaction,

"Well, you get to wear your yellow overalls; I thought I would wear these!"

He didn't know that Tony and Bob had a suit each either, until we rolled into first service and they jumped out of the van in their goldlamé suits as well! He couldn't believe his eyes!

24 – About Piggy

David "Piggy" Thompson was born in a house next door to where he started farming just outside York. He bought a sow or two and built his farm up from there. His Uncle Sydney had a farm and was a bit of an influence, I believe. I think Piggy got it all going whilst he was still at school but ended up being one of the biggest pig breeders in the UK!

He was quite a character and made a very good living from the farm. He once bought this Rolls Royce and to celebrate this purchase he took one of his pigs in for a ride in the back of the car to say 'thank you'!

When he took his last pig to market, when he sold up the pig business, he took some champagne with him to say 'cheers'!

We met when he joined York Motor Club in early 70s and rallied first of all an old Volvo then a Mk. I Escort with a Volvo engine and box in it. The results really started to come when Tony Drummond built him the green Mk. I 1800 BDA CVN 950L. He got some cracking results in that car.

He did the Scottish Rally first year in CVN and got a fabulous result, a top 10 position, 9th overall I think it was, first international rally and first private entrant. He won loads of money (prize money in those days!). They went up onto the stage to pick up this huge trophy; then they would take it back off you! You couldn't keep them!!! You got some little thing to take home!

Roger Clark was doing the British National Rally Championship in those days in his Esso Uniflo works cars and would usually win everything. A lot of the big rounds were in Scotland and they joined up with some of the Scottish Championship rounds. Roger had his own personal mechanic, a bloke called Norman Masters. Me, Wrigsby and Guernsey Tom went with Piggy on every rally so we thought we ought to get to know this Norman Masters as he knew a thing or two about these Escorts and he might be able to tell us a few things.

Well Roger would usually win but there was always a good gang of lads behind fighting for the other positions, people like Paul Faulkner, Robin Eyre-Maunsell, Andy Dawson, Billy Coleman, Peter Clarke and so on but Piggy could always get amongst them and usually had a top ten place by the finish. Anyway we got to know Norman as we would see him in the bar at the finish 'cos the Scottish championship rounds were sponsored by White Horse Whisky (they used to support Gavin Waugh in his Gp. I Avenger too).

Roger often won not just bottles of whisky, sometimes crates of whisky, and Norman usually got some of that. We thought we had definitely got to get to know him now. Anyway we would usually end up pissed with him and we learnt all sorts whilst he shared his whisky with us!

I serviced for Piggy loads of times. By, we had some fun! Mind you, we often spent so much time servicing and chasing about we never got to see any cars on the stages, so I bought a little Monkey bike. I fitted twin seats so me, Wrigsby and Guernsey

Tom could jump on and nip down to see the end of a stage and then dash back up to the barge when Piggy was due! It worked a treat. Mind you it only had about 25bhp, so it was a struggle going up some of the hills sometimes!!!

Piggy fights with a door plate

We were servicing for him the first year this unknown Flying Finn, Ari Vatanen came to this country with his own battered old Opel Ascona in 1975. Cor, it was a mess! When you lifted the bonnet up you could see where the bulkhead was coming away around where the heater bubble was; it was all split away. But he did alright with that car though, he could really pedal it no problem!

Ari had made an impression on the Welsh Rally that year and then came up to do the Scottish. We were in Aviemore and there was this ski slope made from coconut matting and it would wear a hole in your jeans if you tried to slide down it! So we went to the bar and bought two rounds of drinks and said we needed a couple of trays so we could use those! We then had a great time hurtling down the slopes on these trays!!! What a laugh!

Then we found a trailer load of canoes and gets Ari in one of those and pushed him down the slope! He was fastest in that too!!!

On the 1976 Welsh, Piggy had by now progressed to a plain white Porsche 911 which he entered with Alan Greenwood. Very early on in to the rally, Piggy left the road in Brechfa Forest in the dark. He was only two foot off the road, but it was beached and could not get the car back on again!

That year the organisers had discouraged spectators on some of stages and Brechfa was one of them. There was no one around to help them get back on. Anyway further up the stage there was the famous accident when Per Inge Walfridsson had a big off in the Chequered Flag Stratos at a deceptive fire break and rolled. No pace notes in those days of course. The car had burst in to flames and eventually completely burnt out! Fortunately for them, spectators had got into that bend and were there to pull out John Jenson, who had been trapped in that little cockpit and his overalls had set on fire. The car was just a space frame by the end.

We had to wait ages to get in to recover Piggy's car after the delays of the Stratos accident. In those days, it was a huge entry on the Welsh. There were just over 170 entries. Eventually we got in and we came across the Stratos space frame which was completely gone but there were all these bits and pieces of magnesium or something stuck in to the gravel, so I thought I would pick a few pieces up. One of them was the shape of the British Isles and another was like a bloke skiing downhill with a peak cap on. Another one was just a blob! Anyway it is only five years ago since I sold those bits on Ebay to the guy who is the Stratos Owners Club chairman. One of the bits now sits on a plinth as a prize.

Oh, and Ari won the Welsh with Peter Bryant in his first year as a works driver in an Escort of course!

Piggy did the Donegal Rally in 1977; I think it was in the Porsche. Ari and Peter Bryant were in Black Beauty, the David Sutton built tarmac racer (UYY) with Zakspeed type arches on it and won it. There was a party next door to the hotel and getting tickets was pretty difficult. Anyway we all managed to get in. Ari Flatters got in too but poor old Peter Bryant couldn't!! I don't know how the bouncers would take on Bryant, he was a big lad!!!!

I will never forget on the Scottish one year in the seventies, we were having a drink in the bar of a hotel in Aviemore. I went to the toilet, came back to the bar and sat next to this bloke dressed in white shorts and a white polo shirt and glasses. "Now then mate, have you been playing tennis?" says I. It turned out it was Shekhar Mehta!

The famous cannon incident happened on the Lindisfarne Rally. We were staying at The Gosforth Park Hotel in Newcastle. After a few bevvies one night, we decided to move this bloody great cannon out of the Captain's Bar at this hotel and put it on the hotel roof! Don't ask me why, I haven't a clue, but it seemed a really good idea at the time!

We took it up the stairs, in to the lift, through our bedroom window and on to the roof. Guernsey Tom suggested we pointed it at Piggy's window so when he drew the curtains back in the morning it would be pointing straight at him!

Next day, the lady at the bar says, "No one's leaving until this gun gets brought back downstairs!"

Finally, when we gets back from the rally, the receptionists said it took three men and block and tackle to get it back down! I says, "Why didn't you use the lift like we did?"

We went back ten years later when Piggy and I were shooting in Northumberland and the receptionist remembered us! Amazing we didn't get banned really!

On the Mintex that year, the rally was based in Scarborough and we were staying in the Grand Hotel, I think it was. Piggy was in the Porky with Mike Nicholson, I think, this time. Me, Smithy (from Smithy's scrap yard just outside York) and Guernsey Tom was with us servicing. Piggy comes in to service on the Marine Drive and the back end of the Porsche was right low down. Something was definitely wrong.

Somebody said that they fit torsion bars on the back of the suspension from a VW Variant estate car. So Smithy says, "Oh we've got one of them in scrap yard at home." We decided me and Tom would drive back to York to get them in Piggy's Roller! We might as well go in style!

We had already had a few beers when this was decided like, so off we goes back to York. Then we realised the Roller needed some petrol so we stops at Rillington petrol station on the road back to York. Well a couple of scruffy lads in overalls emerging from this lovely top of the range Roller saying, "just put a tenner's worth in," and then scratting around for money; what did we look like?!

So we went to Smithy's scrap yard and took these shafts out, and then headed back to the hotel in Scarborough and carried on drinking! The next day we got up and went to service to fit these things. Well, we hadn't a clue what we were doing! You have got to pre-load them before you put the arms on to get the ride height. Anyway we got it all wrong and just ran out of time, so we had to retire back to the hotel and have champagne for breakfast instead!!

Later we decided to go and have a watch, so we used the Roller to go and spectate! On the run out into the forests, somewhere near Hawnby, we got hit on a hairpin by a competitor in a Chevette doing the rally! Turned out this guy in the Chevette was called David Thompson too! Not a great day for Piggy that!

The Roller was great fun to watch in. There was five of us all having such a laugh!

That was typical of rallying with Piggy, total chaos but in style!

One year we went to watch the Lombard RAC Rally in his road going Porsche 911. We had been down to the headquarters and had a drop of syrup, like; then we went off to Sutton Park to watch. Piggy wasn't 'feeling very well' after consuming a lot of top shelf and spent all the time behind a tree throwing up! He missed the lot; he didn't see one car!!!

Guernsey Tom (Tom Riordan)
25 – Piggy's go-kart madness

Piggy, Yuk and I had a race with a proper go-kart on slicks round his pig buildings at the farm one night in the summer; it was pretty dry, as I remember. It was an Upton Villiers with a brand new engine and it went like stink. I did some work on it prior to us using it, fixing a few problems with the steering.

Yuk and I were on the same second having never driven the thing previously. Piggy was a second faster and neither of us could get any closer to him throughout the evening, even though we all went faster as we got quicker and more daring.

It was obviously quite dangerous as there were vents sticking out of the pig buildings quite close to our heads and there was a really narrow section next to a silo. Yuk and I used 1ˢᵗ gear here but we discovered that Piggy was changing into second on the short straight and chucking it round the next corner. He later admitted that he had been practicing quite a bit before we had our go. At the other end, we were driving over two tracks in the concrete and it was twitching the kart sideways towards the buildings when we went over them at speed. We were probably doing at least 60 mph down the longer straights... madness but great fun!

Guernsey Tom (Tom Riordan)
26 – Rallying with Yuk and Piggy

I think it would be 1974 RAC Rally when Dave Richards navigated our service vehicle, a V6 Ford Transit. Mike Nicholson sat in the hot seat in Piggy's green Escort. Dave R had co-driven for Piggy and was seen as a Wales specialist. I remember waking up in the back of this Transit which was bouncing around a bit to look out between DR (reading the maps) and Yuk (driving) to see two black lines of tarmac, a mountain on the left, nothing on the right and in thick fog; we were doing about 60 mph!! It was quite an exciting wake up and a big short cut apparently!

Another year

Extract: Tom Riordan's report of the 1977 RAC Rally taken from York Motor Club's November Magazine. Piggy had LBO 2P by then, an almost new Gp.4 Mk. 2 Escort BDA bought from Jeff Churchill and had Alan Greenwood co-driving:

Saturday

Set off from York early morning all prepared and revved up to go. Met Yuk at Piggy's farm and picked Wrigsby up on the way. Got onto the A1 (M) and the barge engine boils well and will continue to do for the next five days! Proceed at slower speed for the rest of the journey. Gets down to "the smoke" and Drumbo's service crew pass us and get lost.

Go to scrutineering; can't find Greenwood, so I substitute. We pass the chimney test only after a lot of rude Finns push in. Went to the Wembley hall next; checked for radio and petrol or lack of it. Marshals push us up a ramp into the hall. Yuk appears from the hall where no service crew personnel are allowed, armed with coffee and buns at about £2 a throw. Then a panic erupts as another lot of marshals, about 15, take over the car and push it into scrutineering. The scene is unbelievable; cameras flashing, bright lights, hundreds if not thousands of people looking on, dolly Lombard birds all about and me. I kept tripping up all over because I haven't got my glasses on. I think Yuk knows everybody there is to know because he is still in there with us, wandering about.

The scrutineer passes our car and we are pushed out of the hall, drive back to our park to find Drumbo legalising his hand brake as it is not quite what the scrutineer likes.

Piggy and Tom heading for scrutineering on the RAC Rally whilst Yuk looks on.

After a bit of tyre swapping and generally looking around to see what we can scrounge, Greenwood appears, slightly put out that we have been to scrutineering without him.

Anyway we set off for the hotel and between us we manage to navigate through the London traffic to the hotel.

Sunday

Next morning back at the start, we retrieve our trailer from the starting area causing much upset with the marshals as Yuk is still blowing his police whistle.

The morning's servicing goes well with Piggy's Escort running like a train. We arrive at Towcester race course and find that the service area is a sea of mud. Brookes is trying to get his springs changed and things are getting a bit tense as time is very short. While we are there, a service vehicle hits Robin Eyre-Maunsell's car, much to his disgust.

We run out of petrol near Birmingham just where the Chequered Flag Stratos is in dire trouble. We miss Piggy at the service area so we short cut above Sutton Park, back onto the rally route. Two miles down the road, an awful banging starts so we stop, expecting the worst. "It's alright," says Wrigsby, it's only the prop shaft. A quick calculation reveals us to be ahead of Piggy so we proceed. After a few more miles, the noise getting worse, we find a helpful scrap dealer who chops off the offending end, shoves a Victor 101 prop up the other, welds both together and off we go; perfect. In the meantime, I tell Piggy, who passes by on the road.

We arrive at York on Sunday night, another sea of mud off the concrete at the racecourse. We find Bill Lumb who is going with us for the next two days.

Monday

Monday morning – with snow on the ground, things look a bit grim. Everything is going well except that we have a bit of knocking in the van back axle. As usual, we ignore all noises. It is a fairly quick run across to Great Orme, with a few tarmac stages in between. Now we set off for the forest where the rally will be won or lost. Once into the forest, Piggy is much happier and we hear that Drumbo is having trouble with his electrics, but we don't know what is wrong, so we carry on. Back down on the flat a few miles further on, Wrigsby driving, there is an almighty bang from the back axle. He presses the brake pedal and with three smaller bangs, it goes to the floor. Eventually we stop. We take the wheel off and the brake drum is smouldering. Upon removing the drum, the linings fall off onto the road, the shoes remaining. We clamp up the brake hose and carry on. Predictably, the brakes fail altogether on a hill – bloody auto box won't change down into bottom. We get stopped in a layby just before a rather steep section. We make a more permanent repair (hammer the pipe up so we have no back brakes at all).

Tuesday

Much later, in the early hours of Tuesday morning, I get us a bit lost, as I am dozing off. When I next open my eyes, we are down this narrow, twisty road, with dry stone walls flashing past my face, literally. This starts to frighten and wake me in that order as I realise we have no brakes, Lubo is driving like a man possessed chasing after a Saab service vehicle – and they don't go slowly either. Eventually, we get back en route, the noise at the back is now much worse and wakes Yuk and Wrigsby up. By about six in the morning, we are right at the bottom of Wales and the bearing is buggered or worn out. Piggy's car is serviced and sent off in the hope that they can keep going and we creep on to Brecon. Eventually, we arrive at about 8.00 am, only to find the Vauxhall dealer has gone bust. So we crawl on. After about 5 miles, the van starts to fill with smoke, so we stop to investigate.

The axle is about on fire, so we start stripping it. At this point, our bad luck starts to improve.

The 'help service lads' appear from nowhere in their own cars, just like the firemen. Anyway, one of them takes us to Hereford to get the bits we need. The next time we see Piggy is at Ruthin, twelve hours later. He has been off backwards into a six foot drop, lost three minutes. The spectators lifted it out undamaged.

After Ruthin, we chase back over the M62, back to York. We are on the motorway in thick traffic and the van lights start to flicker and go out. We get Wrigsby to fiddle with the switch. The headlights come on, but the panel lights don't. On the next hill, the engine starts to get hot and blow water from the overflow onto my side of the screen.

We manage to meet Piggy before the racecourse control to change the brake pads and tyres.

Part Two

The continuing saga of Tom's RAC rally or, 'If you want service, don't call us, we'll call you!'

After putting the rally car into Parc Ferme we made our way to John Lavarack's excellent late night RAC tyre swapping service in York. I shunted Piggy back home to bed. Upon returning, Wrigsby and John had fitted the tyres so Wrigsby dropped me off at the hotel for the night for a proper night's sleep.

Wednesday

When I got up next morning, I felt as though I ought to be staying there as I had lost my voice. Some people might say that is a good thing anyway! George Ellis turns up with the super van and drops us off at the race course where we all meet up. Piggy can't get his car started, as the plugs have fouled up and they have to push the car to the start line, which doesn't improve the tempers.

By the way, our crew has changed. Lubo has gone back to work and we now have PC John Wakefield with us. What an enticement for Yuk with his driving habits. We arrived at Croft for the first service and it was bitterly cold. I still had no voice and was feeling dizzy. I think I picked up something in London on Saturday. On the way from Croft, Yuk gets dug into the Policeman's soup, sandwiches and buns, all of which Yuk hands round to us. When we arrive at Stang, it is fairly snowy and the wind is blowing very fiercely. Piggy *appears after a short while and he has had the car on its side. The only damage is on the front wing, which we pull back into place.*

The weather is now atrocious. High winds and the heavens opened on us. We now have a long run in front of us to the Lake District. On the way, we go through floods and give a Frenchman in a Renault some petroleum as he has run out.

The former Jeff Churchill Escort

We miss Piggy at the next service area at the M6 motorway. This is probably just as well as this is another mud hole. I think it is better suited to the African jungle than the M6 motorway. Anyway, we push on to the next service area, which is through Keswick, so with Wrigsby driving, Yuk and I have a raid on the PC's buns, sandwich and soup, much to his disgust! Upon our arrival at the layby, a great big Renault service vehicle pulls up with loads of parts for Renault 5s. Yuk Spares Inc. tries to barter some parts, but they won't play – instead, waffling on in French. Mucky Bob arrives with Guy Lockwood's crew. They look about tired out.

After a while, Piggy arrives. We give him the usual service, one or two odd jobs, send him off and wait for him coming back.

Guy Lockwood appears on the scene and promptly breaks a half shaft, so Mucky Bob has to set about removing it, as we have nothing else to do – we get stuck in and help him. Predictably, it is snapped off in the diff, so the axle comes to bits completely. Mucky Bob and I strip the LSD on the road. As is typical of the Lake District, it is raining somewhat. After a bit, we send them off, but they are about out of time and are to retire after the next few stages.

We progress to Penrith. Piggy comes in and the car is sounding very rough. It sounds as though the engine has had it. Fortunately, it's only a spark plug, but it uses a lot of oil thereafter.

The van is giving trouble again and we have to remove a bit of the exhaust system as it is resting on the back axle.

We set off after Piggy up to Carlisle. A few miles up the road, the van engine splutters to a halt. After a minute or two, it starts again and off we go without any more trouble.

When we arrive at Carlisle, and by the time Piggy arrives, the whole area is very busy and his exhaust manifold is blowing quite badly on the rally car, so Wrigsby is detailed to weld it up and find some bottles to do it with. The night passes fairly uneventfully, except for the van lights flickering on and off most of the time, which makes driving interesting for Yuk and Wrigsby. We are still eating PC Wakefield's grub.

At this time, Piggy's overall position is about 20th and we still have Kielder to come, which we think may cause problems. So, during the service points before, we check the car over thoroughly and send him into this section with three spare wheels just to be sure.

We meet them after the first section and everything is OK. They have seen John Taylor off in the forest. It is now raining very heavily which makes working very tedious. The next service area is on the A68 at the side of the road. It's very busy again with spectators everywhere. Yuk takes the opportunity for a call of nature and promptly stands in someone else's! Many derisory remarks come from him and many laughs from us.

Piggy comes in, having successfully negotiated Kielder with no problems, so we are now looking to the finish, hopefully. The van lights are now getting very bad, with a constant smell of burning coming from behind the dash. A lot of cars move over to let us through, as they think we are flashing at them. I decide that some sleep is required so PC Wakefield takes over the maps to the next halt at Teesside Motel. I awake a bit later hearing someone say we are here at the airport, but why is no one here? Fortunately, we are only a few miles adrift.

Thursday

The halt is a good long one and we get a chance to have breakfast which is very welcome. We leave for the next service after Hasty Bank in North Yorkshire. I promptly get us completely lost as my map seems to be out of date. This causes much laugher from everyone as the only place that I seem to get lost is in Yorkshire. Eventually, we arrive at Ingleby. There are cars everywhere. When we try to go down Hasty Bank to the service, there is a blockage. There are spectators' cars either side of the road, which is not very wide anyway and two lorries have met in the road plus other sundry vehicles.

PC Wakefield emerges from the van, dons his hat and proceeds to shift the obstructions, much to the amazement of competitors and spectators alike. After about ten minutes, the road is clear. Piggy arrives and everything is OK, so we send him off for the last stage.

Our next service area is at the fire tower in the middle of Dalby Forest. There is plenty of action here as cars are coming from various directions. Eklund's Saab appears coming down the road a bit sideways and very bent. Yuk, having not seen a woman for days, is trying to ape Roger Clark's wife in front of Yorkshire TV's helicopter. The helicopter is trying to film the area and is very close to the trees and tower on numerous occasions – must be a masochist! After the servicing here, which passes fairly uneventfully, we progress into the last service on the A64. Here we wash the car down. We send Piggy on to the finish and go back home. I arrive at home to take Janet out, have some tea, sit down and fall asleep."

27 – Yuk's reflections on the 1977 RAC Rally

Piggy always insisted on staying in posh hotels. This particular year the rally started from Wembley, but Piggy insisted in staying in a posh hotel miles from the start. The organisers had started supplying courtesy cars free of charge to get you back to your accommodation, so that was great.

We jumps in to this Austin Maxi and this 'doris' was driving us. Well, Piggy was always a bad passenger – he was useless. We set off in the back of this Maxi. "We'll have to stop!" he shouts.

Missus, pull the car up quick!" I shouts.

He had hardly got the door open before he spewed his guts up in the middle of London!

It were nowt to do with alcohol of course!!!

I was sat in the back of the service van going down to Wales. PC John Wakefield's wife had packed him up with loads of buns and sandwiches. Someone says, "By, Yuk's quiet." I was sat very happily in the back eating all the buns! Oooo, he did bollock me, did John.

"We had better get back to York to get replenished!" he said!

28 – Cheap rallying in a Mini Marcos!

In 1978 I was still selling Mini bits then and still working out of Bill's place. I bought a Mini Marcos and I thought I would rally that.

I made a roll cage for it, made some dural plating for the underside and the sills. A new laminated screen from Marcos was £50. I couldn't afford that.

You would go to scrutineering and the scrutineers would put Polaroid sun glasses on and they could tell whether it was Triplexzone or a laminated screen; "Yeah, yeah, yeah, that's fine, Yuk!"

Well, they must have known it wasn't laminated, but didn't say nowt!

I did the Crystal Rally in it. It cost £32 to enter and I took an Irish lad with me to navigate; well, I didn't know he was gay! We were doing this quarry stage and we caught this Mini up. The road went over this crest. I went to the right of them to get past this fucking Mini. Well, there was this biggest fuckin' puddle you ever did see! The bloody Marcus just hit this puddle and comes directly to a halt... and floated on it!!!

The flying Mini Marcos.

So I says to this lad, "Fuckin' get out and give us a push!" but he wouldn't! Luckily, Billy Ballcock was there with his mates and they pulled us out. We dried her out with some Rocket WD and set off and left the bonnet with Billy! So that is how we got to know Billy Ballcock (Dave Elcock) and his mates, Queer Ken (Ken Hartley) and Irish Pete (Pete Kitching)!

Billy Ballcock (Dave Elcock)
29 – Let's play Dam Busters!

I joined York Motor Club in about 1970. The motor club would meet up at the Dunnington Sports and Social Club on a Wednesday night. Yuk, Ian Oldfield, me and quite a few others would leave the club, jump in our cars and drive in to York to The Black Swan pub for a swift one. We would go from there and head off to Andy Elliott's Hotel where things would often turn into absolute pandemonium!

We would usually end up doing some daft games like Boat Race or even Dam Busters! Somebody always ended up getting wet through!

The Boat Race consisted of a tray of water, about a quarter of an inch deep in a tray with a cocktail stick at one end of the tray and another cocktail stick at the other, with 3 people in a team at each end of the tray. The intention is that one team try to blow their stick from their end of the tray to the other and likewise the team at the opposite end try to blow their stick to the other side!

The tray would be set up on the floor and both teams would be on their knees bending right down to start blowing. Yuk would say, "Are you ready everybody? No cheating now – 5, 4, 3, 2, 1, and, with that, just as everyone starts blowing, Yuk would slap his hand down in to the water covering everyone!

Dam Busters consisted of five seats in a row. The centre chair was the pilot, two engines at either side. You would have a gunner at the rear and one at the front. The idea with this game being that, after several pints, we took our positions on the chairs and make all the right noises and actions as we set off from Elvington Airfield on our way over to Germany to do some bombing.

Then as we flew over France we would be attacked by the Ack-Ack gunners! These would open up, so the audience would all have to go "ack, ack, ack, ack.......," as loudly as possible.

One by one, an engine would catch fire and drop off, so they would be put out (i.e. water thrown over them!). Eventually just one engine would be left with one person left waving their arms about being the sole engine keeping the plane in the air... and the audience still going "ack, ack, ack"...

"Oh no, the last engine has caught on fire! QUICK!"

And this person would have a bucket of water thrown over them! It got to a point where no one would ever join in because they knew what would happen next!!

We did such a lot of daft things, like buying a condom out of the machine in the loos, putting it over your head and blowing it up with your nose!

One night, one of Andy's guests came down in his pyjamas and told us all to shut up as he was trying to get some sleep! Andy never charged him for that night! Fair enough, I suppose!

Sometimes, we would then go on to Ziggy's Night Club in the city to finish the night off! How we got to work on a Thursday morning after that, goodness only knows! When you were with Yuk, something daft usually went on!

One weekend, York Motor Club was running an autotest at Riccal Airfield. Yuk, Golly and I decided we would go down as it was a gorgeous day. I brought my two kids along, who were about five or six years old then. We watched the autotests for a little while and there were loads of people there we knew and the kids knew and the kids were all playing happily together.

Yuk says to me at lunchtime, "Come on Billy, let's go to the pub." So I left the kids playing with their pals and we went down to the village pub for a swift one.

After a while I says, "I will have to get back now. Where are my kids?"

"I think Golly's got them," says Yuk. Golly is in the back room of this pub.

"Golly where are the kids?"

"Don't know!"

Yuk says to Golly, "Go back to the airfield and pick Billy's kids up will you?"

So off Golly goes, only to return with two kids in the car and they walked in to the pub... but they weren't mine!

"Yuk says, "They aren't Billy's! Take 'em back and get another two!"

It almost sounded like, go and swap them for a better couple!

Paul Skinner

30 – The Marcos and the missing wheel nuts

My first memory of Yuk was on the Leeds Crest Forest Rally (held in the classic local Yorkshire Forests) in the late 1970s. I was navigating for Mike Stephenson.

Yuk was seeded one in front of us in the Mini Marcos and he'd never driven it with a helmet on. At the start, he realizes that he could only fit into the car if he tilted his head 20 degrees to the left or right. This was so uncomfortable that he attacked the roof at service and created a dome in it so he could sit upright!

Later in the day as we were waiting for a stage to start, we were all milling around chatting and I looked down at the Marcos's wheels. I noticed it was missing half its wheel nuts!!!

Yuk starts f'ing and blinding about his service crew for over tightening the nuts!! He then just spread what nuts he had around and continued as if nothing was wrong!

Someone asked him, "What is it like rallying this Mini Marcos?"

Yuk's answer was, "Why it's like chasing rats up a drainpipe!!!"

31 – Rally cars borrowed off Piggy

Piggy's Mk. 1 1800 BDE

Yuk lifts a leg on Cottam in Piggy's Mk. 1

Piggy first lent me his lovely, green Mk. 1 Escort CVN to use at a sprint at Cottam Airfield. I had been spannering for him and to show his appreciation he leant me his car for this sprint. It must have been about 1973 or 1974.

Well, I had only ever driven Minis before and this was a completely different kettle of fish! Boy, did it go and handle! It would three wheel everywhere like they did in them days! I came 2nd overall to Paul Stephenson. That set my mind thinking... one day, I have got to have an Escort. But it was going to be a couple of years yet before I achieved that!

The Chevette

Then I got the chance to drive his full works spec Gp.4 Vauxhall Chevette HS on the Cork International from a town called Clonakilty or Clonka-clitty – something like that! Piggy lost his driving licence so he kindly handed the drive to me! We had to use his car and co-driver, so me and Wardrobe (Ian Jemison who built the car in the first place) did it.

The car was virtually brand new and it was first time for me on pace notes, so I was feeling pretty apprehensive. Also, I was under a fair bit of pressure 'cos Piggy had been seeded somewhere in top 10 'cos he had done well the previous year! I didn't want to be seeded there so I asked the organisers to move us down a bit,

Yuk flying in Piggy's Chevette.

so we ran at 35 or something like that. But we still had number 10 on the door.

I couldn't wait to start the race and was getting all worked up, but it got delayed. They were running a horse race up the street and back and we couldn't start 'till this horse race had finished! Most of the spectators were paralytic!

The rally finally got started. Bugger me, we were doing quite well till the last fuckin' stage when I cut a corner too tight and bust two fuckin' tyres and we only had one spare!

I had to ring Piggy up at home afterwards to tell him the damage but he wasn't too bothered and said I could use the car again on the York National!

Next day after the rally, we were all a bit hung over. The hotel didn't have a decent hot water boiler so three of us had used the same bath water and it was freezing cold by the end. One of our service crew called Conrad Blake, a little bloke, wouldn't get out of bed and we wanted to be leaving! We picked him up in his mattress and tipped him into the freezing cold bath. Well, that got him up quick!!

So we did the York National too. Nothing spectacular this time; I don't like crashing!

32 – Yukspeed moves to Gobbo City

Yukspeed Rally Spares was ready for a move by now. I got to thinking it was time for my own place. It had worked out very well at Bill's place at Escrick; we never had a wrong word in over eight years. So, November 1978 I found a place on Elvington Industrial Estate and took my Mini Marcos with me. My new location became known as Gobbo City; I don't know why, it just did!

I had moved onto Ford parts by then. There was a market for them now. I was still selling Mini stuff but then business really took off and within six months I needed

Yuk and Lou retired first time out on the Gwynedd

more space, so I got the double unit next door. There were no contracts in those days, you just talked to the neighbours, did a deal and that was it; £50 a week.

My next door neighbour on the estate turned out to be Sue (Sue Lamb of Solarwall) and we started going out together after meeting up in Ziggy's Night Club in York, Andy Elliott's place.

By 1979 the Marcos had gone, business was still snow balling and I tried a RS3100 Capri for a couple of events. It didn't stay for long though 'cos I started saving up for another Escort!

It would be 1980 when I started building my first 2 litre BDA Mk. 2 Escort. The shell was an ex-Drummond build with a raised floor pan and was painted in the colours of Tony's then sponsors, Hepolite. The car had done only one or two events and then Guy Lockwood had bought it. He was re-shelling her into the very last Mk. 2 Gomm shell ever built and I bought the old Drummond shell off him and put in a 2 litre BDA, which I bought off Dave Oldfield (used to co-drive for Steve Bannister and once a very successful local driver himself in Mk. 1s and 2s).

I did the Gwynedd with Lou Naylor, but retired. Then I did the Mintex but the battery shit itself. The York National came next with Kevin Carruthers and we came 12th, which was some going 'cos there was a hell of an entry. We did the Tour of Lincs, 4th o/a and then we went off to Belgium for the Haspengouw. The battery shit itself again; it was just an old Mini battery and wasn't up to the job really!

The Lindisfarne Rally brought a result which made a lot of people comment 'cos we got an 8th o/a and there were some big names there! So the results were really starting to come and I was really enjoying myself! Business was great, rallying great and Lamby was brilliant! She had started co-driving for me occasionally and we did Sligo together.

That car also brought me my first ever outright win. Huddersfield Chris (Chris Walker) was with me that time and we won the Summer Stages Rally on Fulbeck. It was a great feeling to get that first win. We beat David Bell by 15 seconds and Steve Johnson by 45 seconds and scored 5 fastest times out of the ten. Mint!

I liked winning, so thought I might do it again! A fortnight later, me and Lamby went and did the Ziebart Stages at Catterick Camp and we won again beating Keith Stones and Chris Fishwick by 19 seconds!

Mark "Skids" Skinner
33 – Memories of Gobbo City

I used to visit Yuk at Elvington now and again. I remember when he put the Marcos up for sale. There was a stack of various cars lined up in front of the gravel pit pond on Lavarack's Industrial Estate where Yukspeed was based and, as stocks grew, the Marcos kept moving further forward towards the pond. Every week in Motoring News where Yukspeed would advertise his wares, a comment was made about the Marcos: "Someone come and buy this car... it's getting closer t' pond... it's on the edge...it's gone for a swim!"

One time, me and my brother Paul visited him and he had this very up-market, nearly new Range Rover in his workshop from some local gentry. It was nothing like his usual collection of customers' cars at all! It had a very new, different kind of stereo in it and the customer couldn't get it to work properly. It had six or eight speakers fitted but he could get only the front ones to work.

Yuk had managed to get the stereo out of its housing but had struggled to get the back off as it had special screws fitted. So, he had used a hammer and chisel to get into it. The carpets were up in the car, speakers were out of the doors, wires hanging out everywhere.

"Do you lads know out about these fuckin' things?" asks Yuk. "It's only working out of the fronts and I've been working on the fuckin' thing for two days now!"

We helped him put it all together again apart from the back and then adjusted the balance on the fade and, hey presto! They worked! He couldn't believe it!

Me and Paul nearly wet ourselves laughing!

So, how did you get the name Yuk?

It was through my uncle's name, Yuk Fu Chung. I've got this uncle who lives in China … he runs a Chinese eating house called 'The Rising Sun' but really he is a drug peddler! Anyway, my parents adopted part of his name.

Paul Skinner

34 – Bad Influence

At the time Yuk had his place in Elvington. My brother, Mark, and I would regularly call and share a coffee or lunch which normally consisted of a Pot Noodle or 'shit in a bucket' as Yuk liked to describe it!!

The first week of the UK lottery I called in to see Yuk and he was full of anticipation of winning the great event. We talked about it for a while and eventually he showed me his slip with his selections on it. He'd spent ten pounds and EVERY line had the same numbers so if he'd won he'd have shared it with himself 10 times!!

Yuk was really a bad influence on us. We were over for the Manx Rally and Mark would be maybe 16. He got absolutely hammered with him! That was just the start!

Billy Ballcock (Dave Elcock)

35 – Kick him in the bollocks, Billy!

I bought a second hand Mini for my wife to use and it needed tidying up. I didn't have the money to pay someone else to do it in those days, so I asked Yuk for some advice on what to do. He said bring it down to my workshops and I will show you how to fill in the holes, rub it all down and paint it up. I would go down in the evenings and weekends and I finally got it finished one Saturday morning.

I took my son with me who would only be 6 or 7 years old then and Yuk's black Labrador, affectionately called 'Jimmy Shit' jumped up on my lad and put his paws on my sons shoulders. "Kick him in the bollocks, Billy," shouts Yuk, "that usually does it!"

Wardrobe (Ian Jemison)

36 – They are fucked, Dave!

Dave Bullock had gone out and bought a pair of Bilstein struts and took them over to Yuk's at Gobbo City for his opinion.

Yuk said,"They are fucked Dave!" and threw them in the pond!

Dave was gutted!

Dave Oldfield

37 – £200 short!

Yuk wanted to buy my 2 litre BDA engine for his new yellow Mk. 2 and we agreed a price. This motor was a really nice piece of kit. It originally came out of a Zakspeed Escort racing saloon that Drumbo had bought for the fuel injection system. I bought the engine from him but with milder cams and carbs and used it quite successfully on local events in my newly built Mk. 2. When I broke the car up, Yuk made me a fair offer for it and we agreed a deal.

The day he comes to pick it up he gives me it all in cash and says he is off on holiday and back in a fortnight. When I get round to counting up the cash I found it was £200 short! I couldn't get hold of him, knowing he had gone away so had to wait till he got back (no mobile phones in those days)!

"Yuk, we are two hundred quid short, mate!"

"No worries," says Yuk. "Pop round and I will sort it out."

When I gets there, he hands me a bucket, full of coins. "Here you are kid; that will cover it!"

It wasn't a penny over! He must have scraped together every bit of loose change he could find!

York Motor Club magazine report written by Yuk, August 1981

38 – Off to Ireland for the Sligo Rally 1981

Wardrobe's suggestion:"Let's go to Sligo".

"Aye," says I. "Where is it?"

"West coast of Ireland."

"Jesus, Mary and Joseph! All that way for 11 stages!"

"Aye," says he, "but there's 6 grand's worth of prize money.

"Book me a ferry!" says I.

There was quite a gang of us: Me and Chicken (Sue Lamb) had Golly and Huddersfield Chris servicing for us in the yellow Mk. 2 BDA.

Old Ianfield (Ian Oldfield, brother of Dave Oldfield) had JP (Jonathan Pulleyn) co-driving in Ian's ex-Waldergard shelled blue Mk. 2 BDA (The original GJN 126T shell which Piggy had crashed).

Ian's brother, John and Ian's lovely wife, Christine, were servicing for them out of their old Volvo estate and Wardrobe (Ian Jemison) had his yellow Chevette HS with Dave Boyes co-driving and, I think, the late John "Rupert" Close helped out too possibly, with Bilko (Mike Jackson). I'm sure there were two others, but I can't remember now!

We gets the Wednesday overnight ferry from Liverpool to Dublin. "We don't need a cabin," says Old Ianfield. "We will be propped up in bar all night."

It turned out the bar shuts at 1.00 am! He and a lot more spend the night shouting 'hughie' down the big white telephone!

Gets to Dublin at 7.00 am and sets off for Sligo – 150 miles! We arrive at the hotel at 3.00pm. Golly and Huddersfield Chris empty the suitcases out of the barge while Chicken and me park the racer in the garage. We get back later and Golly says, "Where's your suitcase Yuk?"

I says, "in the barge!"

"It's not," was his reply.

"Must be at home," says I.

By this time Lamby is leaping up and down making funny noises about leaving the case in the hallway to put in the barge. After much stomping about and cussing, Lamby and me go shopping for knickers and shirts and things (like tablets from the doctors). Ever heard of a chemist not selling toggies?!... There's one in Sligo!

Friday was spent fettling the race car and sampling Smithwicks and Guinness. Saturday dawned long before I popped my head out of the window to be greeted by lots of gnats pissin' non-stop!

The race started about 11.00 am after a drivers' briefing where we were told that there were 175 entries and 15 reserves. It was a shame not to let the reserves run, so they were not penalising for early arrivals at stages! Just go straight into the stages and get them over with.

First stage: no dramas. Second stage: 50 yards from the end, hairpin left, got round no problem, then a leprechaun leaps out of hedge bottom and to miss him we went up the banking and got stuck!

Well, who do you turn to when Yuk is stuck?!!! Two dozen Irish lads converged on the car and lifts us back on. Dropped a minute. Crawled out of stage with front wheels akimbo, whistles for Golly on CB and gets 'em down to the stage finish to fix the car. We nibbled 10 minutes into lateness. If we hadn't got the CB we would have been OTL (over time limit).

Third stage, rally leader John Lyons crashes. Second man, Hugh O'Brien passes Lyons. He sees Lyons' car off, gets excited and he goes off 200 yards further on! That left Vince Bonner, who moved into the lead, which he kept 'till the end.

After 7 stages, we were tenth, one second behind eighth place. It had stopped raining by now. The roads were still damp, so we put slicks on, only to get a front wheel puncture 5 miles into the 15 mile stage. We stopped to change it and dropped 4 minutes, which in turn dropped us to 24th overall at the end. Old Ianfield and JP were going well, but they had a couple of offs too and finished 13th overall, 2nd British crew and 5th in class an' all. Wardrobe was 34th overall.

At the prize giving do in the evening, Old Ianfield and JP went up onto the stage that many times to pick up trophies, they got more and more pissed 'till eventually JP falls under the table!

A good time was had by all 16 of us, definitely an event worth doing."

39 – Lou and the flu – snowy Mintex Rally 1981

I don't do dark, but we had to do if we wanted to do the Mintex. It was quite a big event in those days, loads and loads of stages including night stages on tarmac on Otterburn and that particular time it's snowing as well! It was me and Lou Naylor that year in the yellow Escort.

I try hard not to retire on rallies if I can. After all, I have usually invested a lot of money and time getting the car ready for the event. The thought of throwing all that away does not appeal one bit. This particular Mintex was a really tough one, mainly because of the snow and ice. We retired eventually on the rally 'cos I had flu. I was proper sick with it. Lou says, "Oh Yuk, there are only four stages left to do!" but I was knackered! I just couldn't go any further; there was nothing left in me.

That yellow Mk. 2 had a varied history, 'cos at one point I stripped the car down and sold the ex Drummond/Hepolite shell to John Nicholson at Newcastle who still has the car to this day. I then built a new yellow Mk. 2 with a shell from Dave Oldfield keeping the YUC 405 number on the new car. I used that car again very successfully before selling it on complete to Steve Shaw, a farmer from Thirsk with a wooden foot!!! You couldn't make it up, could you?!

I wish I had kept the old YUC 405 number, but I let it go at that point, so Steve Shaw used the car with that plate. The car was white by then.

Eventually Charlie Taylor and his brother Richard had YUC too, doing very well with her in the forests in the 80s with a 2.1 BDX fitted.

Billy Ballcock (Dave Elcock)
40 – From Harrogate... the Mintex started

I first really got involved with Yuk on the competition side when he asked me to go servicing for him on the Mintex International. Part of my job, whenever we set up shop, was to get the artificial legs out and prop them up against the barge! It was also my job to tell people he used to drive in them!

The event started from Harrogate this particular year and, of course, we were to stay over in Harrogate ready for the start. Yuk had booked just one room for the whole crew, which was quite common for him, the idea being that some of us had to sleep on the floor!

The trouble was that the crew was quite big, as he had a chase car crew as well, so there was probably about eight of us in total! We arrived at the hotel, went straight to the bar and got pissed! When I finally got up to the room and opened the door, there were about four televisions in there! God knows how many beds were squeezed in there too!

Somehow, the lads had raided several other rooms and 'borrowed' all these beds and TVs! It all seemed great fun at the time when you are pissed, but in the morning when you are semi-sober, you can't help wondering how the hell you are going to get rid of it all!

Me and Tall Paul (Paul Whitehead) were in Yuk's old Ford Granada estate car which was packed with stuff, so much so it was dragging its arse along the ground almost with the weight of everything! It really needed a castor on the tow bar to stop it digging in!

This particular year, the Mintex headed down to Lincolnshire. Me and Tall Paul managed to drag the arse of this old Granada all the way down there, to the huge old RAF aerodrome called Hemswell. This was to be both a service and a stage.

In the packed service area, we saw the works service crew of Pentti Airikkala using a blow torch to warm up the back tyres of his silver works Chevette; I had never seen that before!

We watched Pentti set off from the stage start which was next to the service area going up one of the little streets that led on to the main runways. Then we set off to look for some space to set ourselves up when, fuck me (!), only shooting down towards us comes this bloody silver Chevette at a million miles an hour!

"Oh shit, we've driven on to the stage!" says Paul, so I threw the car to the left, up a banking, the tow bar digs in to the earth, then we realise it's not Airikkala on the stage but his team mate, Jimmy McRae, in an identical Chevette warming his brakes up! What a relief!

JP (Jonathan Pulleyn)
41 – Haspengouw Rally – Summer 1981

Day One

Three crews from York Motor Club were tempted to try the delights of Belgium closed road special stage rallying with lots of backing from the organisers to tempt foreign crews over to their country. They offered heavily discounted ferry tickets through North Sea Ferries for the rally crews, vans and barges, very cheap accommodation when in Belgium and, I think, free entries as well in those days. This was a big international rally and was part of the European Rally Championship.

Yuk entered in his yellow Mk. 2 Escort BDG with Alf Smith co-driving; Charlie Lamb entered his white and blue Mk. 2 BDG too with Half a Brain (Mick Dent) on the notes. I was servicing for Wriggy (Alan Wrigglesworth) who had Pete Williams in the passenger seat in their white and green Mk. 2 1600 Escort. Wrigsby's sponsor, Barnitt's of York, supplied the matching smart Ford Transit service van and its managing director, the late Ian Thompson, came along to assist and buy the beers!

Charlie and Mick headed off for Belgium early in the week prior to the rally to make their own notes, whereas Yuk and Wrigsby decided to purchase their notes from Simon Everett who was resident over there at the time and offered his notes at a reasonable cost.

We met up with Yuk and his crew (Paul and Golly) at Hull docks to take the whole team on board at the same time. Yuk lost one of his rear lights off the trailer climbing the steep ramps on to the ship, much to everyone's amusement!

Our cabins were located and travel bags deposited, then the bar was found next and the team settled in for the trip across the North Sea to Zeebrugge. Once everyone had tried hard to drink the bar dry, we headed off for our cabins. I found mine but discovered someone had taken it and was in my bed! Despite my protests, this guy refused to give back my room and I was unsure what to do next!

"Well if you are stuck, ring up Yuk!" was often the quote used in Yuk's adverts in Motoring News, so I found Yuk's cabin, knocked on the door and explained my predicament to an ever so slightly pissed Yuk!

"Don't worry Jon, we'll soon sort this out!" and we go off to find a purser to help. Clearly, my room had been double booked, but Yuk not only made sure I got another room but an upgrade too!

The next morning, having arrived at Zeebrugge, we all had a somewhat quiet breakfast on board due to many of the team having hangovers!

Once disembarked, we headed off for the rally HQ at Landen, a small but pretty town beyond Brussels. The town was buzzing already with rally related banners in the streets and market place, mainly with backing from the Belgian cigarette manufacturers, Belga and Bastos.

The HQ was based in Café de Ton, a small cafe in the main street. Once welcomed and signed in we were given instructions as to which hotels had been allocated and how to find them. We headed out to Sint-Truiden first, where Yuk and his team were booked in. We were a bit disappointed we could not all stay together, but there were simply not enough rooms available. We asked the proprietor if he could help, but nothing could be done. We followed Yuk, Alf, Paul and Golly through the main reception, out to the back of the hotel to find what can only be described as a shack in an overgrown yard!

As we entered the front door (of sorts), we had to negotiate between a partly floor-boarded hallway and what was just lino lying on top of the earth! Yuk's bedroom had two camp beds (it was a twin after all!) and a hook in the ceiling to act as the wardrobe! There was a wash basin but it had a part bar of soap in it which had been gnawed at! Yuk reckoned a rat had probably given it a nibble!

The bathroom was even worse. The pipework was held together with tatty, rusty looking jubilee clips but the pipe had a split in it so it was going to leak anyway! Every time you flushed the loo you could have a shower at the same time from the leaking pipe!

Ian fell about with laughter at the state of the place. Wriggy and I looked at each other in sheer relief, thinking how lucky we were not to be staying there now! Yuk's hotel was costing 500 francs a night (which would have been about £6.00 then). I couldn't help thinking what was our hotel going to be like then at 460 francs!

Twenty kilometres down the road, Wriggy, Ian and I arrived at Hasselt to find our little hotel was basically a bar/cafe with rooms. This place seemed to be open as long as people were there, which was basically all night! Upstairs, I found the room I was to share with Pete Williams who was travelling separately and joining us the next day. The door had a six inch gap at the top and bottom, the floor was filthy and there was even broken glass all over the carpet. I cleaned the bathroom up as best as I could using Swarfega from the van and had a good go at picking up the broken glass! I tried out the bed which was so old my backside touched the floor! Still, the consolation was that we at least we had floors in our rooms, unlike Yuk's team!

That evening, Yuk and crew drove over and joined us for supper and drinks and decided understandably to stay with us, camping on our two bedroom floors.

Day Two

The following day, Pete Williams arrived and the drivers and co-drivers headed off to check the notes and get familiarised with the stages whilst Ian and I worked out our service schedule and checked out the locations. The road timing was going to be tight. We realised preparation was key as we would be working under pressure to get to every service on time.

The evening was spent trying out Hasselt's bars and cafes. The food was ok, the laughs even better!

Friday was scrutineering and the start of the rally too in the evening. Scrutineering took place in a large sports hall and a spectacular affair it was too! All the roads leading to the hall were closed off so only rally traffic could enter. Down this long street were rally cars, barges and caravans (no really large motor homes in those days to speak of) along with endless food stands supplying sausages and chips with mayo. The Belga and Bastos promotion girls were everywhere giving away free ciggies, stickers and so on.

The process of being scrutineered was very quick. Wriggy and Pete were completed in around three minutes! They didn't even look in the boot! Of the top crews there, Patrick Snyers was at one in a plain white Mk. 2 Escort Jeff Churchill hire car costing, we understood, about £1000 a day plus tyres (seemed a lot of money then!). Jimmy McRae was at two in an Opel Ascona 400, Guy Colsoul was in another Ascona 400, Robert Droogmans at five in a Belga-liveried Tony Maslem hired, fuel injected Mk. 2 Escort.

Willie Rutherford (RIP) was entered in his ex-Toivonen Escort with Brian Harris; Bertie Fisher (RIP) in his ex-works, ex-Billy Coleman tarmac spec Mk. 2; Bohne in a Mercedes automatic; John Buffam in his ex-works Triumph TR7 V8; Chris Lord's ex-works Talbot Sunbeam plus lots of other interesting tarmac rally cars, mainly Porsche 911s and BMWs. All very tasty!

Early evening saw the cars fired up and brought out of Parc Ferme into the warm evening air and to the start ramp in the town square, where thousands of eager spectators thronged. The atmosphere was akin to a Formula One race meeting.

It was time for Ian and me to rush off to first service which was directly at the end of the first stage. As we waited for Wriggy and Pete, Yuk and Alf came through and all was well with them. We could see they had been trying hard as Yuk's front discs glowed in the dark as did many of the top runners. Then it started to rain, really pouring down! The roads suddenly became very slippery as the slick racing tyres struggled to cope with deep puddles of water. Wriggy and Pete arrived; the driver's side front wing was pushed right into the wheel arch but clear of the wheel and headlight pointing skywards! They had been caught out on a fast left which turned from smooth wet tarmac to cobbles and the car left the road hitting a tree.

Quick repairs were made and they hurried off to the next stage. Time was very tight. Ian and I pressed on to the next service, but then got caught in a long traffic jam in the dark. Impatient rally crews overtook all the stationary traffic sat on the right-hand side of the road, desperate not to lose road time only to end up being stopped themselves and blocking the road completely. A British crew had been 'T-boned' at a road junction by a non-competitor and carnage was everywhere. Finally, we got through and reached the next service in a small town in the early hours.

Haspengouw

The atmosphere was electric. Spectators watched the crowded service area as crews rushed in and out tight for time, some competitors driving over tools and tyres in their haste.

Yuk arrived covered in sweat, looking strained and not enjoying the darkness at all but otherwise all was well with the car and crew. Charlie was next and again all seemed well. Wriggy and Pete arrived next and needed a quick plug change, but were otherwise fine.

In the next lap of stages all this changed for our team. Both Yuk's and Charlie's cars flew in and out of service without problems, but Wriggy and Pete were late coming in. The last stage that night was 14 km in the dark, and Wriggy's alternator failed and the car came to a halt once the battery had gone flat. Unable to coax the car any further, a marshal offered them a loan of the battery out of his road car, mid-stage. They came rushing out of the stage and we dived into the van and found a spare alternator, but it hadn't got a pulley on it, so we had to remove the one off the broken one. By this time, the crew were right out of time and our efforts had been wasted. We were all gutted, especially Wriggy. He was an auto electrician by trade and felt a little embarrassed too! Ahem!!!

York National Rally in the TR7 V8

On Wykeham North with Lou – Ginge looks on in the blue jacket with red flash above

About to leave Barton Hill

Otterburn at night

Circuit racing could be fun!

*One of the auctions
at Barton Hill*

with Malcolm Wilson

Early road rally days

Mint shot of one of the G3's

Lambton Park with Sue

Early morning on Millington Pastures

Donegal with Bill Lumb

Classic black and white shots on the Mintex

Both Yuk and Charlie were still running strong until Charlie appeared with the car looking somewhat worse for wear... they had rolled. It was held together with bungie straps and tape all over the place and a plastic windscreen. They had gone flat over a crest on a straight, hit a bank on landing and the car flipped, landing on Charlie's side on its nose and front pillar! This stopped the stage whilst the car was put back onto its wheels. They had been just one second in front of Yuk at the time and were having a great old battle, and now they were out too. Just Yuk was left now and the second night halt gave chance for everyone to grab some rest and take stock before the final day.

Day Three

Day three was another beautiful, warm day with blue, clear skies. We all went off spectating and saw Yuk through a special stage which included an industrial estate and he was flying – neat and tidy but very quick. The pace at the top end was incredible and Yuk decided to just keep it safe and see who else might fall over or go off.

In the end, not many more did, and Snyers won from Jimmy McRae with Ian Grindrod second, Colsoul next, Droogmans fourth and Rutherford a popular fifth. Chris Lord grabbed eleventh, Derek Boyd was seventeenth but our biggest heroes, Yuk and Alf, came in twenty fourth overall and fifth in class which was a very respectable result when you look at the company they were in on a big European Rally Championship rally. There were 143 starters and just 74 finishers.

The Sunday night celebrations were quite something. Two Belgian fans of Yuk's were keen for us to visit a night club 'where it's at' as they put it. We all piled in to Charlie's Range Rover (about eight of us) and followed these guys about 8km out of town, pulling up in a dark street outside a house with just one light on.

"Mmmm, not too sure about this," said Yuk. "Fuckin' hell, it must be a whore house!"

Some of us were not too sure how to react! Anyway, after a bit of discussion it was agreed we would move on to some of the pubs in this village, which turned out to be great and we continued our journey of discovery finding a Volvo parked in the loos of one pub! Don't ask, I don't know why either!

We sat outside one pub which had a swinging door. Golly went inside to buy a round and came back with a full tray of drinks only to stop and have a scratch between the swinging doors, dropping the lot!

We listened all night to stories of the rally, including Alf's pace notes which he read out to Yuk:

"Fast right over crest, absolute left, fast right and for fuck's sake slow down!"

42 – The Ex-works TR7 V8 arrives!

The TR7 V8 was twitchy!

I bought this ex-works TR 'friggin' 7 from this bloke. When I went to collect it, there was a problem with it; the prop shaft was loose! Luckily, I took my trailer! It was a genuine works car, supposedly ex-Per Eklund.

It was a good car, but it took some getting used to. It's not like an Escort at all, low slung and huge power. Very twitchy. I have never been the fastest driver; I am just a clubman who enjoys his rallying and I'm usually a little bit behind everybody else and steady away. But I rarely crashed or broke the car. I got a few results with it but it was never my favourite.

Eventually, that car ended up with Chris Birkbeck, who made his mark in it and did a lot better than me with it!

Apparently, when he was a kid he used to dream of rallying a car like this and had a poster on his bedroom wall of this very car! Little did he know then that one day he would actually own the bloody thing!

43 – Yuk co-drives for Malcolm Wilson!

I had put an entry in for my local rally, the York National in 1981. It was a year after Malcolm Wilson had damaged his ankles on the Scottish in a big crash.

I had cancelled my entry 'cos I had run out of cash. Malcolm wanted an entry as he had built himself a brand new car and was trying to get back behind the wheel again and see if his ankles could stand up to a day's rallying in the forest.

In those days, you could swap three things: your car, the driver or the navigator, so we agreed to change the car and the driver and I would co-drive. So, I cancelled my entry and Malcolm took it instead. This was quite a big deal for me.

So, there we are next day. I am shitting myself! Malcolm Wilson, star man; Rothmans works driver; brand new Malcolm Wilson Motorsport built Gp. 4 Escort with a Terry Hoyle engine it; Pace/ Autosport National round! There were all the top national drivers there like Malcolm Patrick, George Hill and so on. Fortunately, there were no pace notes to worry about, so all I had to do was hang on to my seat!

Well, we got to about the third stage – Pickering, I think, and we were about 14 seconds in front. We knew that 'cos they used to write your time down at the stage finish and we could see where we were.

Yuk Hodgson with Malcolm Wilson. Malcolm was given the drive on condition he took YH as co-driver on the York National.

Malcolm and Yuk pictured in Rally Sport magazine

So, we sets off down this stage and I'm trying not to brake with my right foot against the navigator's foot brace. We go flying round this right hander into a fast left and, fuck me, Malcolm misses his braking by about a split second! The car climbs this bank on the outside, falls over onto Malcolm's side and slides back onto the stage on its side!

"Right Malc, don't move. I am going to open this door at the top of my head here," I says.

So I undid my belt, stood on the side of the transmission tunnel, pushed the door up and fell out of the fuckin' thing, but with me legs still stuck in the fuckin' door and belts, and I'm hung upside down! Finally, I managed to free myself and dropped down on my fuckin' head!

We ended up blocking the bloody stage so they had to stop it. We finally got sorted out and drove the car out of the stage and we retired. I hurt my shoulder a bit, but we ended up in pub anyway. It was The Moorcock Inn somewhere up on the top of the moors. We got some sandwiches and drink ordered and Malcolm sat down munching his sandwich when this local yokel walks in.

He says to me, "What you been up to?"

"We've been rallying, like," I says.

"Ahh, have you? There's loads of good lads round here."

I says, "Have you heard of that Malcolm Wilson?"

"Oh aye, I know him, he's a rum lad i'nt he?"

I said, "Yeah, and have you heard of that Yuk Hodgson an' all?"

"Oh yes, I know him," he says. "He's a rum bugger too!!"

Poor old Malcolm nearly choked on his sandwich!!!

Now, I learnt so much sat with him that day; it was either flat out, foot to floor or on the brakes – nowt in between. Total commitment!

I am not a quick driver me, but I have learnt a lot from top people like Malcolm. I learnt a lot from Piggy too, like dabbing the brake with left foot over brows to keep the car steady. He learnt that from top co-drivers such Mike Greasley who had been with professional lads like Pentii, who was leading the RAC Rally in '76. You can learn a lot listening to others.

Huddersfield Chris navigated the chase car on this rally. He couldn't believe how professional Malcolm's team were. The night before the rally, they asked Chris to join the team meeting where they discussed which tyres to use for each stage; they were asking questions like was the forest surface loose or hard, smooth or bumpy and then working out the right compounds! Not like our approach which was stick some cheap Colways on and let's get going!

44 – Yuk's biggest win – the Quip Rally 1982

In the summer of 1982, I sold the TR7 and wanted to get back to Escorts. I never really got on with the TR 7 so I bought a right nice car which came on the market, NWR 184V – a Mk. 2 Gp. 4 Escort from Fred Brown who owned Tip Top Stores. This car had been built brand new by Drumbo (Tony Drummond) and was hardly used.

I got some great results with it. We won the Holderness; got 5th on the Lindisfarne (which made a few people sit up and notice) and 3rd at Lampton Park. Then came the Quip in October which then was part of the very popular and very competitive BTRDA Championship.

Lots of top crews were entered like Clinton Smith in his Malcolm Wilson-built Escort, as was Darryl Weidner's Mk. 2. Dennis Moody was in his BDG engined G3. That year's Gold Star Champion, Trevor Smith, was in his Mk. 2, there was Fred Henderson in his Chevette, Steve Benton, Trevor Prew, Banner of course in his new Escort (soon to roll into a ball again!), Phil Taylor and Vince Wetton – all in Escorts too. There

was even a brand new Quattro which appeared that Ron Hudson was debuting. You can tell how well the organisers thought we were going to do 'cos they seeded us down at 17!

To be fair, there were quite a number of the

Quip Rally, Yuks biggest win with Phil Shaw

top lads dropped out as the day went on but me and Phil Shaw, who was co driving, didn't have a clue how well we were doing. The rally had been flat out all day and we had not had time to talk to people and find out how we were doing until the very last stage.

There was a hold up when they found a car with a body in it, so they had to shorten the stage! Whilst we were queuing up to start, I got chatting to a few of the top lads and one of them says, "It looks like you are leading, Yuk."

"Get out of it, that can't be right!"

We didn't even have a service crew that day!!!

Of course, in those days, there were no notes, but Phil was good. If we were going into a right hand bend and it was opening up or tightening up, he would say clearly what was happening. I could let the car drift out further or straighten it up accordingly. He knew the dangerous places and would tell me in plenty of time... but not too early. That is how we attacked the stages 'cos we weren't using maps or owt.

So it was down to the last stage, between me and Dennis Moody in his G3, and we won by just 1 second!

It was a magical win and a fantastic after rally party in Scarborough that night!

Quip Forest Stages Esso /BTRDA Championship Round 7 Results

1. Yuk Hodgson/Phil Shaw 2.0 Escort RS 54m. 48s

2. Dennis Moody/Andy Graham 2.0 Escort DM 3 54m.49s

3. Clinton Smith/Stuart Dytham 2.0 Escort RS 55m. 10s

4. Darryl Weidner/Doug Hart 2.0 Escort RS 55. 16s

5. Fred Henderson/Fi Beacon 2.3 Chevette 56m. 57s

6. James Sutherland/Mark Atkinson 1.6 Escort RS 56m. 52s

7. Alistair Sutherland/Steve Perez 2.6 Chevette 56m 57s

8. Chris Stoddart/Stuart Thomson 2.3 Kadett 57m. 29s

9. Trevor Smith/Steve Bond 2.0 Escort RS 57m. 31s

10. Alec Cannon/George Tindall 2.0 Avenger 57m. 59s

Motoring News put on their front page:

"Hodgson, just."

"Victory on last weekend's Esso BTRDA Gold Star Rally Championship qualifier. The Quip Forest Stages win went to local Yorkshire ace Yuk Hodgson, driving his Escort RS. After a day long battle in the Yorkshire forests, Hodgson was only able to gain a solitary second lead over Dennis Moody (Escort) whilst over 20 seconds behind in third place came Clinton Smith (Escort RS). This year's Gold Star Champion driver, Trevor Smith, suffered a time consuming puncture early in the day relegating him to 10th place, whilst star of the day was Stafford's Ron Hudson debuting his newly acquired Audi Quattro."

It was very satisfying. I have only ever rallied off my own bat, never had any big sponsorship or any advisors helping out, just did my own thing when I could afford to.

In the end, I needed the money to move to Barton Hill, so I sold NWR to Pete Slights. That car went on to do very well in Pete's hands once he got Bob Sunter's business, Direct Windows, backing him and he really made a name for himself in it on the British national rally scene in both the BTRDA and Shell Oil's National Rally Championships.

45 – Piggy buys the famous works Escort GJN 126T

I remember when Piggy bought this car off Ford at Boreham. I even have the letter from Peter Ashcroft framed in my hallway at home. I bet (Dave) Watkins would kill me for that!

It was the last ever Mk. 2 to be built by Boreham for Bjorn Waldergard on the 1979 RAC Rally. They were testing the new RS 1700T by then, to take it over into the then new Gp. B era. Waldergard had finished ninth in it after all sorts of problems like a bent axle and a few offs. GJN, POO 505R and another one were for sale and advertised in Motoring News in a block advert.

So we went down to Boreham to look at this car in Piggy's Porsche road car. Cor! It was dead special going down to Boreham, but looking at the gate going in you wouldn't think it was anything special.

We met up with Mick Jones and Peter Ashcroft. There were racks and racks of spares all over the place and I noticed a Fiesta with a Mk. 2 floor pan in it too which caught my attention.

Anyway they offer all three cars to Piggy and he wanders off to think about which car to buy. GJN was almost brand new but left hand drive and was £17,000 which was a huge amount in those days! He decided on GJN and I says, "Why buy this one?"

He says, "Well, it will be worth more on a T plate than a R plate."

So he goes to see Peter Ashcroft, who says, "Piggy, you own that car now."

There were no spares with it apart from a steering rack and 2 spare wheels! "Fuckin' 'ell, is that it? We can get those in the fuckin' Porsche then!"

So I says, "Jonesey, what are you doing with all those crates of works spares?"

Jonesey says, "Give us a bid".

Piggy whispers, "What's going on here?"

I says, "Will you go halves with me?"

He says, "Yeah, yeah, ok".

He had just spent £17,000 on a car – what's a few 'undred now!

So we settled on £700. I still have the receipt somewhere for 'misc. spares.' So we spent £350 each.

Jonesey says, "Are you going to take 'em now?"

"Fuck off, we only have the fuckin' Porsche with us!"

Piggy says, "You drive the Escort home, Yuk."

I says, "A left hooker, full works Escort all the way home! No fuckin' way!"

It cost him a fortune in petrol!

46 – Peter Ashcroft and the pig

I had to go back a few days later to get these spares we had bought, so I went in my old Range Rover. Piggy says, "Oh, will you drop off this pig for Peter Ashcroft when you get there?"

"Aye, alright," I says. "Is it alive?"

"No, it's boxed up," he said!

So, I put it in the back of the Range Rover and set off down to Boreham. Anyway, this pig is all butchered up and cut into sections and I thought, Ashcroft won't miss a leg surely so I put a leg under the seat for myself!

Of course, what happens? Ashcroft rings Piggy up afterwards saying, "Thanks for the pig – very nice. Was it a disabled one?"

Piggy says, "No, why?"

"Because there was a leg missing when we got it home!"

47 – Bits of GJN live on forever!

When Piggy got GJN home, he had it converted to right-hand drive by Ray Quinn (former mechanic to Tony Drummond who had set up on his own.). Piggy debuts the car on the York National with Mike Wood and was going really well 'till he upturns it on Cropton and wrecked the shell first time out! Disaster!

He orders a brand new shell from Gartrac and he and I head down to pick it up. They put the shell on the wrong way round on the trailer and the fuckin' doors taped up to keep them shut. Of course, what happens...? The fuckin' driver's door flies open as we are going along, creasing the wing and wrecking the door! What a mess!

He didn't keep the car very long before he asks me to sell it. I end up selling it to a completely unknown driver called John Brown through contacts with Fred Henderson. John turned out to be a real star in that car and did really, really well. His Dad was David Brown Tractors so there was no shortage of financial backing!

Whilst John had the car, he had a spare engine built for it by Terry Hoyle with fuel injection fitted. I had just bought PSG 461P and somebody tells me John has this engine tucked away, so I goes up to Peterlee to this industrial estate where he has all these bits stored. I couldn't believe it! There was all sorts of consumables: complete fully floating Atlas axles, suspension bits, Minilites by the dozen, tyres, exhausts... everything. After a lot of haggling, I managed to do a deal and get the engine with a few other bits and pieces and loads of goodies too!

As it was, I couldn't get on with the fuel injection so I sold that to Richard Moore for £1000. He was rallying a right nice Mk. 2 then. He later sells the fuel injection to Spug (Duncan Stead) who was running him then. Many, many years later he sells it on to Charlie Taylor, who eventually brings it back to me and asks for £5k for it!

"Fuck off Charlie, I had it once and sold it for a grand. Why would I want that back again for five grand?!!"

First event with this Terry Hoyle fuel injected BD was the much hyped Champions single venue rally at Oliver's Mount, Scarborough. All the top local Yorkshire lads were there. The press make a big deal about it all as Piggy had entered in his brand new lightweight Porsche 911 built by CC Racing, and then there was folks like Andy Elliott, Pete Slights, Ian Oldfield, Warren Philliskirk, Bilko (Mike Jackson), Richard Moore, Jeff McNeil – all good lads, and me, all in identical Gp. 4 Escorts plus Wardrobe (Ian Jemison) in a brand new Chevette HSR, all capable of winning. It was going to be nip and tuck!

It turns out the race is between Piggy, me and Andy Elliott. Every time I came down to the Mere Hairpin, we could tell there was nothing in it. Then I goes and makes a mistake and goes the wrong side of a bollard at the split and drops five seconds! I'm now doing everything I possibly can to get that time back. I made up 2, maybe 3 seconds back but just couldn't do any better than that. What a brilliant day!

Piggy won in the Porky, Andy Elliott grabbed second and we were third. Poor old Oldfield with Jim Goodman besides him crashed his brand new Mk. 2 in to the cafe at the top, doing his car no good at all!! You can see some of the pictures in Jim's book 'Flat over Crest- Bang'.

Finally, I get to buy the whole car (GJN 126T) a few years later, in September 1986. The car had ended up locally again, this time with Charlie Lamb. He had used it a bit locally. I bought the car from him with about 20 odd tarmac tyres and rims with it and I stripped the car for parts. When I get the engine, gearbox and axle out and stripped down, I looked at the shell. It was two shells welded together with square turrets in the back! So it wasn't the Gartrac back end, which I hadn't realised at the time. It didn't matter as I already had a good shell at home. So I sold the shell on and kept the registration number GJN 126T and just transferred it on to various Escorts I had over the years.

That plate sat on a lot of cars – Mk. 2s and G3s, but eventually I sold the plate when I decided Escorts had finally had their day in 1993 and bought my BMW M3. I did alright out of that deal for the GJN plate and documents, but I wonder what it would be worth now?

John Forrest

48 – Having a dance with Lionel Blair

At the finish of the Welsh Rally one year Lionel Blair, the famous TV dancer and personality, was at the prize presentation in Llandudno. He was quite keen on rallying and was co-driving for someone at that time who was rallying a Triumph Dolomite.

Anyway, Yuk meets him and they ended up doing the waltz on the dance floor afterwards... brought tears to your eyes!

49 – Yukspeed moves to another pub!

By 1983, me and Sue had been living together for quite a while. We decided it was time to get our own place where I could run my business from. Sue has a good business head on her.

We looked around for somewhere suitable, when fuck me, The Black Horse comes on the market – where I was born! Sue says, "Shall we buy the Black Horse?"

I says, "No way, I was born there. I don't want to fuckin' die there!

Anyways, there was no room for a workshop so we plumped for where I am now at Barton Hill, just off the main A64 Leeds to Scarborough road, which was also once a pub called the Spitalbeck Inn. So, I ends up living in another old pub anyway!!

I had to sell the rally car to fund the move. I missed not having a rally car when money forced the car to go. Competing is good for business; it keeps the name in people's minds and you are always meeting potential new customers. But also rallying, especially in somewhere like Wales or Scotland, is just so relaxing after a hard week working on cars, buying and selling parts and talking to customers. To be able to load up the car on a Friday afternoon, take a good team with you and set off for Wales for example, get there, get through scrutineering then have a few beers, is brilliant... and then the fuckin' rally gets in way! After the rally finishes, it's back into the bar for a proper good session again! You can't beat it!!!

When we were looking for a new home and workshop, we came to see Barton Hill. It turned out the spot was owned by a guy called Alan Jackson. He was one of the lads out of our village where I was born!

So we bought the place in 1983 and got moved in – 30 years ago! It's an old coaching Inn from the 1800s. It's been added to, with an original stable block at the end for the visiting customers to keep their horses! The little road outside the house was the original A64 road to Scarborough. Later, a new section of the A64 was built further away from the pub, which was to be the first dual carriageway to be built in England.

After the war, the name Spitalbeck Inn was transferred to a new building up the road and my place was re-named 'The Old Spitalbeck Inn'. In the deeds to my house, it says, "You shall not let rooms or sell alcoholic beverages," so any bugger that comes to stay, I can let 'em stay but I can't charge them for a room or for any drinks I give them either!!!

The old stables are now my showroom and office. When we bought the place, we knocked through the stable block and built a 40 x 45 foot workshop which Piggy helped me get organised. Loads of people came and helped out. One lad, Colin Popplewell, was a digger driver then. He would dig out the footings on an evening for me and I just paid him back with bits for his rally car!

The business has certainly evolved. It's important to keep in touch with business as it changes over the years. When rally videos first came out, I created a video club. I bought a load and hired them out. I made a couple of dollars but nowt much from that. Trouble was, I would buy at retail and sell them at trade!

The rally spares continued to grow in Ford stuff, but in the early nineties a lot of different cars were coming into the sport like Cossi two wheel drive then four wheel drive, Lancia Integrales and so on, and more people were moving away from Mk. 2 Escorts, but the job was still good, like. I was still buying and stripping Escorts, but a lot of the top lads were moving on. Sierras, Mantas, Metro 6R4s and then early Escort Cosworths. So, things were changing.

Brian Bell was running a Metro 6R4 at that time and was promoting Skegness on the front of his rally car and on his barge. I thought that was quite a clever idea, so I promoted 'Barton Hill' on my rally cars too, to get the message over that we had moved to a new location and called the business Barton Hill Racing, but never dropped 'Yukspeed' 'cos that has been around for ever!

I still sell lots of rally parts now. Things have changed so much over the last ten years in particular, due to the internet. I used to rely on customers selling me their spares which gave me my stock, but now I can buy them on the internet, of course. Parts I sell on the internet sell themselves on EBay and on websites. There used to be a lot of dealers like me around, folks like Pete Stansfield of Yorkshire Rally Spares who now specializes in motor bikes instead.

When computers started to go into people's homes, I realised I needed one too. I remember Piggy saying, "What are you doing with a computer? You can't read or write!"

He was quite impressed when he saw how I was doing business on it! I have to thank Mick Penrose for that. It took six hours sat with me to teach me how to use EBay and the interweb properly! What a star!

EBay has changed, of course. You have to put your minimum price on now and the site is saturated with sellers. If I have got things for sale at whatever price, other people are doing the same. But I run it as a business whereas 'Jack the Lad' can do the trading on the side and doesn't have to pay the Inland Revenue. That does piss me off sometimes.

I manufacture a lot now. I make some panels, fibreglass dashboards for Escorts, Escort fibreglass panels, body repair panels; I just have to cut my cloth accordingly. I am still doing flocking which goes very well too. Business has changed a lot over the years. I am always looking for new ideas.

A lot of my customers have been very loyal and some have become great friends over the years. I have had some famous names ring me up for bits too, including the late Colin McRae, who was working on a Sunbeam at the time and needed a few bits and pieces.

Billy Ballcock (Dave Elcock)

50 – Well, that's fucked it!

Around 1985 Piggy was looking to pair up with a permanent co-driver who was prepared to do a very full season of the then Shell Oil's National RAC Championship and the BTRDA National Rally rounds and even mixing in the odd International rally too.

Yuk very kindly put my name forward, which was really good of him. Piggy was now taking his rallying very seriously. He had a beautiful lightweight Porsche 911 built by CC Racing in Kirkbymoorside, so lightweight even the con rods were made of titanium! He had employed a full time mechanic (Pete Fiddell) to look after the car and a very professional approach was being adopted.

The contrast, co-driving in a team like this compared to Yuk's approach, was enormous. Piggy would have as many illegal services as he could to swap tyres for brand new ones. If we could change tyres after every stage, we would do. He would insist I kept a close eye on fuel levels so we did not carry too much, to save weight. We would test tyres to work out which tyres worked best on different surfaces and so on.

Piggy and Billy Ballcock in the lovely Porsche

The approach contrasted with Yukspeed. Yuk would say, "well that one's better than that one so we will stick that one on, and how much fuel is there in that jerry can?... Ok, fill it up!" With Yuk, you would go down the day before to help him clean the rally car up and load the van; Piggy would pay for someone else to do all that!

Yuk's tactics were always; we will go steady up to the first stage and then wait for 5, 4, 3, 2, 1, Go! And then go like fuck!

Well, the season with Piggy was really producing some amazing results with this car and we were really making people sit up and notice. We were having a tremendous year's rallying.

Then the Border Rally came up, a BTRDA round starting from Gallashields, and Yuk was servicing for us. Still no pace notes so I was reading from the map once again and Piggy was really trying. Piggy did not want anything shouting to him unless it was something you knew for definite, but otherwise he preferred to drive on sight. Any junctions that were arrowed, he could pick up himself; he did not want anything saying.

We came round a corner and came across a clearing of trees. Then we came to a brow which we attempted flat in third. I guess we could have been doing something in the region of ninety miles an hour or so. At that point Piggy said to me, "Is it?"

I said, "yes."

We flew over the brow and we were airborne... as the road went right! Beyond the brow was a tree line which we took as being the road, but it wasn't! As we came down, the car went right but the tail flicked out and hit a tree stump and sent the car into the air landing on its nose, then over onto its tail, then we dropped something in the region of 200/250 foot, eventually landing on Piggy's side.

Me, being the fat bastard I am, the car then came down onto my side... everything went very quiet... and all I could here was the fuel pumps! I switched them off quickly and said to Piggy, "Are you alright?"

There was no reply.

I went for the door handle but that had disappeared in the crash. I looked at Piggy who was clearly unconscious and decided to kick the door open. I didn't want him to see me kicking the door as this car was his pride and joy! I went round the other side to pull him out, undid his seat belt and he came round... we were both really dazed, but Piggy was all over the place... he didn't know what day it was, what rally it was or anything so he got taken off to hospital but later discharged himself when it was clear he was fine.

Sadly the Porsche was a complete write off.

As Yuk said,

"Well that's fucked it!"

Piggy hired a Phil Collins Opel Ascona 400 for one event. It was good to "get back on the horse" as it were, but my heart had gone out of rallying really and I retired from competition after that.

51 – Rallying with Rocket!

We had a hell of a fight on the Sherwood's of Darlington Christmas Stages. The roads were so icy and we were up against Warren Philliskirk, Mike Taylor, Les Graham, Ray Cook, Richard Hemingway, Steve Smith, Steve Magson, Chris Pearson and Dave Turnbull. Lots of good lads all capable of winning. Anyway, after a tricky day just trying to stay on road, me and Suzy won from Dave Turnbull, Maggo and Chris Pearson. A very satisfying win that one.

The local press headlines on the sports back page read:

> *"Hodgson and Lamb win easily*
>
> *Yuk Hodgson and Sue Lamb (Barton on Hill) received a late Christmas present yesterday when they won the Christmas Stages Rally in their Ford Escort RS by a two minute margin. Hodgson managed his impressive performance in freezing conditions and snow showers......."*

Winning at Christmas, Yuk and Rocket!

It was great competing with Sue and we had loads of laughs and quite a few wins together too. We never fell out when competing, just enjoyed ourselves. Little did I know that one day our daughter would be co-driving for me!

52 – Yuk in a box

Yukspeed Rally Spares has evolved as the years have gone by. Nowadays I rely such a lot on the internet and EBay, but when we first moved to Barton Hill the phone was so important and *still is!* Every week I would have an advert running in Motoring News with all my latest bits for sale and I would wait for the phone to ring.

This was a story Motoring News ran in 1988;

> *"Yukspeed proprietor Yuk Hodgson has recently been trading from a Yorkshire village telephone box, although this is only a temporary arrangement!*

Clients have been 'phoning the wrong number ever since MN's classified department published an incorrect telephone number for his rally spares and accessories business two weeks running! Nevertheless, as 75% of his trade is mail order, the extroverted Yorkshireman soon found an ideal solution to the problem and employed a young lad to sit in the 'phone box and transfer the calls. In future, they should phone 0653 81540 and not the coin box. Apologies for all the inconvenience caused by Mr Michael Ellis at Standard House and the advertising manager should be out of intensive care within a week.

Sentember 1st. 1988. No. 124   Yorkshire's bri

NEWS-NEWS-NEWS-NEW
WS-NEWS-N
NEWS-3
NEWS-NEWS-NEWS-NEW

YOUR STARS
32

Dear Angela, Page 8

Why Yuk had to call for help

TELEPHONE

An invitation from

Spange

To enjoy a glass of wine at the introduction of their
Autumn Winter Collection

YUK Hodgson's office is making a temporary transfer – to a village telephone box.
Twice in a national paper – a bible for motorsport fans – his number has appeared wrong.
Yuk, whose rally spares business base is at Barton Hill, near Malton, said: "It turns out to be a telephone box in Westow."
And to save his customers going down the line he called up the Jobcentre to recruit someone to sit outside the kiosk to take the calls.

British Isles, and people are ringing me up all the time.
"For my next advert I said for God's sake get it right – but it came out today and it's wrong again."
"If the 'phone isn't answered I'm losing money so it is worth my while to have someone sat there."
Yuk asked Malton Jobcentre to come to the rescue and to find a recruit to sit by the kiosk for three days.

Number

Yuk in a box!

89

With Yuk currently busy building an extension to his premises, his next rally won't be until the Quip National when he will once again wheel out his Opel Manta 400."

I had to go to the local Job Centre in Malton and arranged for this lad called Tom Pitt, who was described as an ambitious job finder, to sit outside the phone kiosk in Westow village to take the calls! He was a good kid and did a good job.

53 – Yuk gets arrested!

One of the difficulties in this trade is buying from people you don't know. I would never, ever buy anything which I knew was stolen. I don't work that way, I couldn't live with the pressure.

In May 1989, just after we got the new workshop built, I had been buying some stuff from some lads in Hull – things like wings, bonnet, doors, bootlids off Mk. 3 Escorts. One day, I got a knock on the door. It was the day before the Bank Holiday.

Two local CID lads from Malton said, "We would like you to help us with some stolen parts."

"Yes," I says. I thought they wanted me to identify what the parts were or something like that. I am dead against any knock-off stuff. So they cart me off to Malton and say that there is some CID coming over from Hull and they went and put me in the slammer! They take my watch off, my belt and so on. They didn't caution me, but I just couldn't take in what was going on!

Then these other CID lads arrive from Hull. They sit down and interview me. There was the smart guy with suit on and a tough guy with tattoos all over him! They ask me where I buy my bits from, who are my competition etc. and then say, "Have you bought some bits from some lads in Hull?"

"Yes," I says. "I have actually".

I must have done half a dozen deals with them.

He says, "Did you know it was stolen?"

"No I didn't."

"I put it to you Mr Hodgson that you knew it was stolen".

I said, "How do you work that out lad?"

"Well, I've got four written statements signed from these four people".

I said, looking him straight in the eye, "Well go back and get the truth out of them 'cos I do not knowingly buy stolen goods. I can make enough of a living without buying knock-off gear."

I explained – *if* I was dealing with stolen goods, I wouldn't be dealing from the Spitalbeck, would I? I would be dealing on airfields and lay-bys, wouldn't I officer?!"

I was really starting to worry now, 'cos I hadn't made a phone call or anything to my solicitor. I explained I still had some bits left like Recaro seats which I had bought off them and they can come and have a look.

So, we gets back to the Spitalbeck and these guys are in the stable block looking through stuff. There were these piles of empty boxes which had come from the TV Centre in Malton. These had been packaging for TVs and video machines.

"Where are all the TVs and videos then?" they ask.

"If you come with me now officer we shall go and see Gavin who owns that business and he will tell you I get them off him to pack my parts to post them to customers.

So then they ask if I have any more rooms. I say yes and open up my huge 40 x 45 workshop and what's in it? Four Mk. 3 damaged body shells! Well, their eyes lit up and you could see them looking at me thinking we've got you now!

"Well, where is all the trim and stuff out of them?"

So I explained what I was doing – turning them in to rear wheel drive for rally car purposes. I had bought these shells off Simpsons Salvage. If they had just got the sense to ask me, I had a yard long print off from the computer for these body shells. In fact I still have the receipts now, but they had wasted so much of my time now I was starting to feel pretty fed up! So they take all the chassis numbers to check them up (I knew that was going to be ok).

Then they ask, "Any more rooms, Yuk?"

By this time we were on first name terms. They knew they had nowt on me and I knew I had nothing to worry about. Then this fat copper sees a wooden shed down the bottom of my garden (which I have full of old tyres and engines and stuff) and starts wobbling off down there so I shout out, "You want to be careful down there, lad; there are rats the size of cats in there!"

He picks this stick up and is holding this door open with the stick looking all worried and his mates are pissing themselves with laughter!

By that time they are all on my side, but they ask me to go back again to the Police Station so it's back in the Police van again and all the neighbours are wondering what is going on!

Back in the interview room, they ask to go through a book of photos and I pick them out no problem. Turns out these lads had admitted to taking 54 vehicles!! Anyway, they got time for it and I was not involved anymore, thank goodness.

54 – Pay up Mr Team Manager!

We were out watching the Manx in 1983 and we were coming down this road section when we saw Konrad Bartelski. He was the new young up and coming driver at the time, driving a works Citroen Visa (he was once Britain's most successful World Cup downhill ski champion). He comes out of a junction and just slightly touches a non-competing car that was on the main road.

We stopped to help 'cos this Konrad needed to be on his way so he didn't run out of road time. Me and Piggy sorted things out with this lady and a Police officer and we gave her some cash to repair the damage. Later on we catch up with this driver and he says, "Oh I have not got any money you will have to see the boss!"

Eventually we find the Citroen team boss.

"Come on pay up, Mr. Team Manager, you owe us!" That upset him!

It might have been the same year or maybe the year before we were talking to Tony Fall in service. He was running the Rothmans Opel rally team then and he says, "It has been reported that Henri Toivonen has had a puncture".

When the car came in it was obvious the only reason he had a puncture was 'cos he had hit a fuckin' wall!

55 – Yuk goes circuit racing

I thought I would give circuit racing a go when Piggy and I heard about this new rally car class being incorporated into the circuit championships. Piggy had the Starion and I had a Mk. 2 which I had just bought a Millington built 2.2 BDX for. I had been sat on the bog one Wednesday, reading Motoring News and I saw an advert for this motor with Roy Millington: "Just rebuilt, million brake horse power, four and quarter grand!"

I rang up Roy Millington and went down on the Thursday, bought it, came back, put it in on the Friday and my first circuit race was at Oulton Park on the Saturday!

We gets to Oulton Park. It was a bit racey was this engine, double L1 cams 'cos Roy had built it as a racing engine.

I didn't know about this tyre job. You had to use these Firestone road tyres 185/660. They were a fucking awful tyre at the time, hard as nails, they were. The tyre smoke and the black lines I laid down were unbelievable! Sideways everywhere!

So I did practice, which was 15 minutes long. I didn't realise at the time that was to determine your grid position! No fucker told me that, so I got bored after a few laps and pulled into the pits and parked car up. I gets out and there is a bloke stood by the barrier and we start chatting.

He says, "Are you that chap in the blue Escort?"

"Yeah, why?" I says.

"Have you done much circuit racing?"

"No, why?"

"Well, you seem well sideways going into Old Hall!"

"Well, yeah that's what us rally drivers do when driving blind."

It turns out the bloke I am talking to is Jeff Goodliffe of British Vita Racing. "Oh, pleased to meet you!" I says. It was like meeting Keith Duckworth – a God like figure!

It turned out he was looking after some Mk. 3 Escorts that were being raced.

He says, "Nice meeting you. Please go steady; you are frightening me to death! You seem to know what you are doing, you keep coming round again!"

Sideways always seemed to be the approach I took, admittedly not always the fastest way, but definitely the most fun!

Had I realised that I could have practiced for longer, I could have been further up the grid!

For the race, I said to the lads swap the rear tyres from one side to the other. I forgot to tell them that one wheel had inserts too far in and needed a spacer on, so the spacer had to go with the wheel. I went round on the warm up lap and could hear the wheel wobbling about. Tiddles was spannering, so I had to pull into the pits and Tiddles had to get the jack out and sort it out. Tiddles (Pete Fidell) then says, "Off you go."

But I said, "No I'm going to wait until they come round again."

I was going to wait at end of the pit road, but Tiddles says, "No the red light will be on!"

I set off onto the circuit then slowed down to make a race of it! I got such a bollocking for doing that!

There was Cyril Bolton in a Metro 6R4, Piggy in the Starion and Steve King was in the Manta! Of course, I am in the middle of them! Steve King was not too impressed with me, though!

The next race was at Mallory Park; I got a bollocking there as well! This time for kerb hopping!! "Come on you rally lads, keep off the fuckin' grass!" The weekend was a bit frantic. We went for a curry on the Friday night after getting pissed, of course, "Come on John, give us hottest one you've got!"

I told the lads to be at my place at 6.00 am the next morning, not five past, but six. Well, this curry... I have never in my life... when you're pissed you just eat anything... next morning at 6.20 am, I am still sat on the bog wishing I could have my throat cut! The lads are all outside waiting... so eventually I managed to get down stairs and into the van. We just get on to the A1 and I need the toilet again!

We stop at a little service station and I goes and borrows the keys for the loo... well my arse is on fire!! Finally, we gets down to Mallory and practice is on... and all I could think about was finding another bog!

"QUICK, QUICK," I shouted to the marshals. "Where is the bog? Get the fuckin' door open!!"

Anyway, the racing went ok. I think Pete Slights was having a go in his Direct Windows Escort BDA. I decided to take the hairpin on the handbrake; nobody can get past me then 'cos I'm all sideways and look out of control!

I never really understood circuit racing, straight lines and apexes and things!

I did Cadwell Park and was third after qualifying. Howard Patterson was first and I think it was Chuck Nicholson who was second.

I says to Howard, "You and me, let's make a race of it... you know, let's muck about a bit."

On the start line, I think I will have a go at them 'cos I'm on a short diff and little race tyres. We set off and the road curls off to the left. There is a Lotus in front, then Chuck, then me. Then the road starts to go right and I think I will have a go at passing Chuck here on the outside, but he did the same to overtake this Lotus, so where am I going to go? It was either hit Chuck or fuck off on the grass! The road went right and I was scrabbling about on the grass and everybody went past!

So I get caught up again and get past Howard, then I thought I would let him pass me... so we go up 'Mountain' and up to the chicane and Howard goes straight on into the tyres on the outside of the corner! So I pulled up! "COME ON!" I shouted!!!

So the commentators are wondering where the hell we are 'cos we didn't appear... then we come scurrying around the corner! Well, that was my experience of circuit racing!

Autosport; Cadwell Park Report April 1986:

> "Three cars battled it out long and hard. Yuk Hodgson eventually taking third overall from Ian Stansfield and Howard Patterson. Hodgson never took the same line twice up the Mountain but always came in to view sideways!"

Motoring News Donington Report July 1986:

> "Hodgson drifted and opposite locked a little too much on occasion......."

I tried my hand at Rallycross too, in the Mk. 2 Millington. I put 15 inch wheels on and she didn't half lay the rubber down, but I had to chuck the car around a bit to unsettle it before bends! So we get to the race and I did alright. This lad with one of the smaller engined Rallycross cars says, "By, you brake early for corners, you do!"

I says, "Oh, do I?!" I looks across at what car he has and says, "Well, your car probably only weighs about 3 bags of 'taties – my old fucker weighs a ton!!"

"Ah, sorry. I never thought of that!"

I also did a grass track day up at Hunmanby near Filey. I won that in my G3! That was good fun too.

56 – The Opel Manta 400

The decision to buy the Manta came after I did the Silva Stages. John Morton beat me in a Manta 400 he had borrowed off Ian Holt. I bet him £5 that I could set a faster time on the final stage and he beat me!

I bought the Manta off Pete Slights who had hardly used it. It was the ex-Jimmy McRae AC Delco car WIA 5958. The deal with Pete was he would co-drive on the first event and tell me how to drive the fuckin' thing! It was totally different to an Escort. It was all new to me. We had entered the Quip. I picked the car up on the Friday and we took her up for scrutineering, ready for the rally the next day having never driven the car before.

Yuk and Pete Slights try out the Manta

We went straight into the first stage on the Saturday. Well, I have never had so many spins! I was waltzing into the corners like you would an Escort and we ended up waltzing too much and going backwards past the junction I wanted to be up!

It took Slightsy a while before he decided to

tell me, "No you don't drive it like an Escort, you don't throw it at a corner," like I was doing. He says, "What are you doing?"

I says, "I haven't got a clue, you tell me!"

He says, "I tell you what you are doing wrong. You are driving it like an Escort; you should drive it more like a race car – straight line, hard on the brakes then turn into the corner."

You could just drive it in. There was no understeer. If you had to, you could just use a quick tweak of the handbrake but most of the time you just turned it in and it would go. By, it was a nice car to drive; I did enjoy it.

Rally Sport magazine report of the Quip Forest Rally (Marlboro National Rally Championship) November 1987:

> "Car 25 Peter Yuk Hodgson/Peter Slights. 2.4 Opel Manta 400 (Yukspeed Rally Spares). Yuk's first time out in the new car (which used to belong to the co-driver) and it was definitely treated with kid gloves! Unlike his previous Escort, he felt that he really had to drive the Manta and finished 26th."

It caused quite a bit of confusion for the motorsport journalists as Piggy was also out in my Mk. 2 BDG which carried the GJN plate by now! Rally Sport said this:

> "Those famous Yorkshiremen were at it again on the Quip, throwing everyone off the scent of what was really happening. Yuk Hodgson appeared in the ex-Pete Slights Opel Manta 400. Pete himself was planning to enter in his new MG Metro 6R4, but ended up in the co-driver's seat of his old Manta with Yuk. "He's the only co-driver I've ever listened to!" When he was asked if he had actually bought the car, he jokingly replied, "No, but the price keeps coming down all the time!" Meanwhile, Yuk had allowed Piggy Thompson to drive his Escort, although Piggy maintained that he part-owned the vehicle anyway. He reported that the tacho, amongst other things were failing, and claimed: "It's all Yuk's parts which are breaking, mine are all ok!"

Yuk then replied, "Between the three of us, we don't know which car belongs to who!"

Come on lads, get yourselves sorted out!"

One of the advantages of driving an Opel at that time was the Vauxhall/Opel bonus money you got if you won a restricted rally. You could win yourself £500!

We did the Cartel Clubman's Rally and we were having a right good fight with Pete Wells in his G3 Escort. When it came to the night stages, I knew we were going to lose loads of time 'cos, as always, I struggled in the dark. This was made worse by the fact that Pete Wells was an ex-road rally man; he was going to be extra quick once the spotlights were fitted!

Sure enough, as soon as it gets dark he starts taking loads and loads of time out of us, maybe three or four minutes. So I have a word with him, like, what with him being a car dealer, he is bound to take two hundred and fifty bucks and says, "Look, Pete, if you back off and let me win you can have £250!!"

"No, I can't," says Pete, "because of my sponsors!" I thought, fuckin' hell, I've never met a car dealer yet who wouldn't take two hundred and fifty bucks for doing nowt!

So Pete whooped us!

The worst thing about the Manta was how it went in the dry when it was dusty. The doors being all lightweight and the car having perspex windows, dust used to get into the car really easily and everyone was getting their lungs filled up with dust. On the Plains Rally it was so dusty I could hardly breathe! I asked a prominent female co-driver of the time if she had anything to help. She promptly went into her handbag and produced a spare pair of knickers – perfect! I wrapped 'em round my face, over my mouth and over me crash helmet like a turban! It worked a treat!!!

I sold the car finally to Brian Price in Brecon, South Wales, who used it as a hire car and he immediately hired it to Ian Oldfield via Kevin Curran! Ian ended up towing the car down to Wales to use on the Bridgend Stages Rally and then handing it over to Brian Price at the end of the rally!

57 – The Escort G3s

I tried three different versions of the G3 in the late 80s, all rear wheel drive conversions. I was trying to trade in the Genesis versions, so I bought some damaged shells from Simpsons Salvage and made them into rear wheel drive, thinking that Mk. 2s had had their day. Most people seem to think the same then.

I bought a G3 off Martyn Harrison to rally with a BD fitted. I tried all three cars and they were all crap!

Either the cars were not set up correctly or summat, but they weren't right and I was being beaten by people who shouldn't beat me.

So I decided I needed to get back to a Mk. 2.

58 – 'Ginge' gets a squirt!

Nigel 'Ginge' Cay has done a bit of driving and a bit of co-driving. He had been out of the scene for quite a while and he says to me he is ready to get out again. I says, "Do you want to sit in, Ginge – for the York National? It'll cost you the entry fee."

"Yeah, yeah, I'll do that."

He is a right good lad, a real good laugh, so I wondered what could I do to finally get him back after he soaked me once at the motor club years before. Then I came up with this idea. It was the G3 I had at that time with a BDG fitted and it had the screen washer bottle behind the co-driver's seat... I know I thought, I'll T-off it a washer pipe, run it along the intercom wire, run it into my old full face helmet, through the lining to the top of the helmet so it comes out on the crown of his head!

I tell Booler (Derek Parling) and the rest of the service crew what the plan is but to keep it quiet from Ginge. Luckily, the rally was fairly dry so I didn't need the washer bottle too much.

Anyway, on the first stage we are flying, until suddenly we hit this huge berm at the side of the road at a junction! It had been created on a rally some months previously when the route had turned left at this junction but this time we were going straight on. We leapt into the air and the fuckin' car lands in this shallow ditch on the outside! It took us about three miles to climb back onto the road. We finally get to the end of the stage and I says, "Fuckin' 'ell Ginge, wasn't that cautioned?"

He says, "Yeah, yeah, yeah, but you were going too fast; I couldn't keep up!!"

So when we comes into first service, Booler says, "Have you given him a squirt yet?"

"No, no I haven't yet!"

Next stage we arrived at the stage start and I thought I will just give him one little squirt. He says nowt.

Went to the next stage start and I give him another little squirt, a little bit longer this time. I looks over and can't help but giggle. My wipers are going and the window is washing;

He looks across and says, "Why are you washing the windows they don't need doing?"

I says, "You shut up and mind your own business!"

I gave him a right good squirt this time and I saw him digging out a tissue and wipe and dab his maps and paperwork; 10 seconds, 5, 4, 3, 2, 1 and I am pissing myself!

We get to the next stage and I give him a right good dose this time.

He says, "Yuk, there is water coming out of somewhere on to my maps!

So I says, "Well, make a note for the service crew when we get in and they can take a look."

We went into service and I tell him to ask the lads to put some tape around the hole where the aerial is on the roof. I see Booler as we arrive in (and none of lads have said anything).

"Put some tape on the roof 'cos Ginge is getting a wet back please."

We leave service and we go on to the last few stages for the day. It is still a bit dry so I think I might as well finish off the bottle now, so I give him a right good dose!

"Yuk," he protests, "look at all this fuckin' water!"

I said, "Well, did you tell them at service?"

"Yeah, yeah, I told them."

... and there was water dripping off his chin!

Anyway, we get to the last stage and I decide to empty the whole bottle on him! There is water everywhere and he hasn't a clue where it's coming from!!!!!!

We get to the finish at Ravenscar and someone finally spills the beans to him. Everyone has heard what we have been up to. Booler (he is one of the instigators) asks me if I got him? I said I emptied the lot on him!!

Come the presentation and we have won the Clubman's Rally and, of course, an award and I was asked to make a speech. All the audience are applauding and laughing... so I think ... great I have the crowd on my side, little knowing Ginge has got a soda syphon in his hand and he is about to soak me!!! Boy, did he drench me!

Gingespeed (Nigel Cay)
59 – Ginge gets a squirt – right to reply

Never let the truth get in the way of a good story, but in the case of Chapter 58, it was all true – well nearly!

He did forget to provide the important reason why his plan was hatched, which takes us all back to 29th July 1981, a Wednesday, a national holiday to celebrate the Charles & Diana's wedding. This was all thanks to Yuk's favourite Prime Minister, Maggie Thatcher (and he has seen more Prime Ministers pass through than most of us). I know it was a Wednesday because it was York Motor Club's club night at Dunnington Sports Centre.

We had all had the day off. Drinking had commenced earlier so spirits were high and Yuk was holding court and made some smart-arsed remark about me, so I boldly reached for the bar soda syphon and pointed it at Yuk in a bit of brinkmanship. Yuk immediately responded very confidently, "Ginge Speed – you would not dare!" Never dare a twenty year-old!!! Splosh! Too late! He got it and was well and truly soaked! He just wiped himself down, smiled as he was way too drunk to retaliate and said, "One day Ginge, one day, one day Ginge!" with that special Yuk type sparkle in his eyes... and as they say, the rest is history... well Chapter 58!

So, back to the rally. He may have wished I paid the entry, but he actually only got half and petrol, not a penny more! The rest was great factual recall by the Old Git! We did have a rain shower which diverted my suspicion of water entering the car and before anyone who classes themselves as an accomplished navigator starts giving me a hard time for missing the caution, transferring from driving a mildly tuned Mini Clubman rally car to the awesome power of a BDG in a lightweight G3 was not easy. I have to confess, I was not ready for it! Trust me, I was just about to call, "Caution!" when we hit that yump absolutely flat in 5th gear and it really did feel like 3 miles in the ditch before we scrambled out!

of Dalby on Sunday and after all the internationals had gone through the tracks were already in a bad condition.

It did not help things that the roads were still as they were after the RAC Lombard Rally. They should have been repaired but the heavy winds and large snow falls meant that no work could be done.

Some of the local hopefuls were Yuk Hodgson and Nigel Cay, from Malton Motor Club, Ian Jemison and Dean Kellet, from York Motor Club and Charlie Gabb with Jon Riley from Selby Motor Club.

The going was tough and only 22 drivers finished out of 44 starters.

One of the retirements was York Motor Club's Steve Adamson with Richard Jackson, his co-driver.

They broke their exhaust in the first Wykeham stage which caused them to nearly fail the noise level check at Scarborough. They managed to repair it at the service point, thanks to some on-the-spot welding by John Hodgson.

But the necessary repair restricted the exhaust which in turn kept their times down.

Olivers Mount at Scarborough was particulary bad: "When we were going downhill the car was fine, but going back up the hill I could have made a cup of tea we were so slow," said Jackson.

After a valiant effort the pair eventually went out on the return trip to Dalby. This dashed the hopes of the other two drivers in their team of lifting the team award.

The award eventually went to Selby Motor Club who were the only club to have a full team of three finish.

The drivers were Charlie Gabb, Stephen Eeles and Andy Johnson. They finished fourth, 17th and 18th respectively.

The fourth place drive by Gabb was particularly impressive as his car was a standard Toyota Corolla GT and he managed to stay in touch with the winners who were all driving specialised cars.

The Trophy was won by Geoff Tunnard from Licolnshire, but the local boys put up a good show.

Yuk Hodgson finished second on the day but was then moved down into third after receiving four minutes of penalties. This put Ian Jemison, in his rear-engined Vauxhall Avon, into second with a time of one hour 33 minutes and 30 seconds.

Jemison's remaining team mate, Phil Acomb with Judith Littler, finished in 19th in their first rally in the Vauxhall Nova, prepared by Jemison. Their third man was Adamson.

Yuk Hodson's team mates, Simon Redhead and Jeff Scrivner, both retired but the Maltons Club had four other finishers, three of them in the top ten.

York only had the two finishers and Selby four.

The event was a great sucess all round and all clubmen thoroughly enjoyed themselves, even though the start was before daylight on the Sunday.

Although there were a few complaints from villagers living within the rally course area, the organisers said that the rally went very well indeed.

So well in fact that there is talk of it returning to York next year.

Above: Car 217...Ian Jemison and Dean Kellet, after their second place in the Talkland Trophy event.

Left: Yuk Hodgson with co-driver Nigel Cay congratulating each other after finishing third, despite a hefty four minute penalty.

Yuk and Ginge make up!

Finally, the Old Git forgot to mention in his chapter that we set off from the start line of a stage with the hydraulic handbrake on, and the 270bhp trying to spin the wheels was truly a sight to see!

So as the Old Git mentioned, water was now not dripping but pouring like a small stream which could have watered three Somalian villages!

Ah well, as my moment of fame draws to an end, I feel duty bound to tell of one final incident which occurred after the shenanigans which went on at the prize presentations/ after rally party.

I was in the Gents. It is important here to picture a long 5 metre back wall (15 ft for the farmers and anyone from Beverley!), with an old-fashioned floor level trough urinal. Got it? Good! Yuk stumbled into the Gents himself... wobbled to the far left hand side – 'pissed' (in both senses). As he turned to leave, he dropped his left foot into the trough (like a bike wheel in a tram track) and then traversed the whole length of the urinal not able to lift his foot out! Finally I hawked him out and back to the bar!

So the moral of the story is that the person that gets you into a ditch flat in 5th may also be the person who can get you out of a urinal trough!

I have to say it was a real pleasure and certainly an honour to have sat next the legend which is Yuk!

60 – Lost in Europe with Piggy

Davos

It would be April 1989. Piggy says, "Come on, let's go and watch the Monaco Grand Prix. We'll go the week before and get a bit of skiing in Davos in Switzerland then wobble down to Monaco for the Grand Prix."

We went in his short wheel base Shogun. We set off from Hull to Zeebrugge then we drove down to Switzerland, then on in to Davos. He was keen to go there 'cos he had been with his wife Barbara and son James. Thing was, it had been a real mild winter and there was hardly any snow so the ski resorts had a pretty miserable season.

We checked into our hotel and Piggy says to the chap in reception, "Can we get some skiing in?" but we are told, no, it will be the end of the season that weekend and they were about to close down.

So Piggy says, "Can you get us a helicopter?"

I thought, fuckin' 'ell, a helicopter! What is he going to do now? Is he going to get us dropped off at the top of a fuckin' mountain glazier for us to ski down?! He was as crap as I am at skiing; it was never going to work – we'll be dead!!!"

I says, "What are you doing?"

It turns out that hotels have a certain number of bedrooms to let for the season. There was no snow in Italy; France hadn't got any snow either so they were limiting the number of people who wanted to fly into Switzerland.

The hotel guy says, "Even the Queen of England couldn't fly in when she wanted to without prior arrangement!"

He was a bit strict this guy! Anyway, to get rid of us this guy says he had heard there was loads of snow at St Moritz and to drive down there. Well, I had no idea how far that was or how we were going to do it. I hadn't got a clue.

That night we went in to a club in Davos; what a beautiful club it was. People were very laid back, beautiful women behind the bar – they were a million dollars! I was well taken up with this. It was a bit bloody posh for me mind! Davos is the hub of the bloody posh people i'nt it?!! Mind you, I had a white jacket on and a bow tie so I think I looked the part!

There was this bouncer there. A great big lad, about 6'12", Swedish, and built like a brick out house, he was.

I said to Piggy, "We had best make buddies with him, 'cos looking at all these boxes of beautiful whiskies, we might end up in trouble tonight!"

I get chatting to this lovely lady called Sonia behind the bar, "Excuse me love, how many different bottles of whisky do you have?"

She says, "Eighteen!"

... and they were posh ones too, malt whiskies and what have you.

I says, "Will you bring them to our table please, we would like to sample them?"

So she comes over to our little table with nine napkins and nine glasses and puts a glug in each glass.

Piggy asks, "What's going on here?"

I just says, "Don't worry about a thing!"

Thing was, Piggy knew his whiskies and knew what was good and what was not so good. So we tried each one tasting them carefully.

Then I says, "Right Sonia, let's try the next nine please." and over she comes, clears away the first lot and brings in the next nine!

Piggy says, "What's going on?"

I says, "Don't worry about it; it'll be alright at the end of the day!"

We sampled eighteen different whiskies! Eventually Piggy drags it out of me. "I told them you had inherited a castle in Scotland and we know nothing about whiskies so we decided to go all round world to try different ones and learn all about them!"

"You bastard!" he says, "You'll tell folks anything!"

Eventually Piggy goes off to his room for the night and I stayed up a bit longer before finally deciding to head back to the hotel myself. Somehow, I had found the rear entrance to the hotel and got in a lift up to my room. I get out at the top and I'm walking down the corridor to our room when I saw this naked bloke laid out on the settee on the landing! I thought fuckin' 'ell, I am not going to look at this bloke! It were only Piggy completely bollock naked – fast asleep in the corridor! God knows how he had got there!

Next day we leave for St Moritz in search of more snow. We sets off and Piggy says, "Which way?"

I says,"Not a clue. Follow that road down there".

As we drove out of town, the snow was really, really high. It was about 12' high at the side of the road but there had hardly been anything where we wanted to ski!

A bit further down the road, we realised we were running out of fuel so we pulled into this petrol station and it was pay with card only. Well, in those days we didn't have a card; we just did everything in cash. So we set off again... but wait a minute, who had left petrol cap on the roof of the car?!

We drove down to the next little town and saw a workshop at the roadside. There were service bays, doors wide open and cars on ramps, but nobody about! Deserted! I thought, is no one going to serve us? It turns out the whole of Switzerland closes down for two hours for lunch time. They had gone to the local hotel for a bit of lunch!

So we went and joined them, got some beer in and a bit of lunch and waited till we could get some fuel bought!

We could then carry on with our journey down to San Moritz. We found a hotel and – brilliant – they had loads of snow!

Next day, we went down to the ski hire place and sorted out some kit, then got in the lift with a few others and up to the top where it was all misty. Everyone gets out and goes to the left but for some reason we goes to right. Off we set down this mountain; it was mint. No-one was in our way and we both flew down. Being the end of the season, the place was to ourselves virtually. We goes and gets one or two of those Irish coffees with a nice drop of whisky in. Then off we go again up to the top, and back down for more Irish coffee!

Piggy then says, "Are we off back up again?"

I says, "I tell you what Piggy, I am not sure we can stand up now mate let alone ski back down. Let's just stay here now!!!"

Milan

Finally, after a few days of this, we decide to head off for Monaco. We get into Italy somehow with my map reading and, against all good advice, we end up by mistake in Milan! Everyone we spoke to had said whatever you do don't get stuck in Milan traffic, stay on the outside but we forgot, didn't we?! It was traffic chaos! We were stuck for hours! Still, it didn't matter. The advertising hoardings in Italy are almost pornographic so that kept us amused for hours!

Monaco

We finally get into Monaco and Piggy has booked us into a lovely mega hotel with millions of stars to the west of Monaco called the Carlton in Beaulieu-Sur-Mer.

First night, we are all dressed up for a posh night out at a hotel restaurant called La Reserve I think, which was within walking distance and I am back in my tux. This old bird turns up outside the restaurant in a Mk. 2 Jag and I am stood in the hallway. She hands me her keys and says, "Park that up will you, young man." Piggy is howling with laughter! So I goes and parks it up for her! Well, you have to do what you are told don't you?! Anyway, I got a tip so that was fine!

In previous years, we had been to see the Grand Prix with our good mate Diesel Jack who would just turn up, but we never knew when.

If you ever go to Monaco you must go to places like Flashman's Bar and Rosie's Bar where all the old racing drivers used to go, like Graham Hill, Mike Hawthorn, Brabham, Fangio and Stirling Moss (there are photographs and autographs on the wall in the bar).

On this trip, the first night we are in Monaco we popped into Flashman's Bar for a few gin and tonics. In places like that you run up a tab and pay at the end of the night. This particular night we were about to leave and Steve who runs the bar and has got to know us from the year before had said to us, "Where is Diesel Jack?"

Piggy said, "He could turn up, we don't know, you just don't know what he is going to do!"

At the end of the night, we'd had loads of gin and tonics. We asked Steve how much we owed and he said, "Oh, sort it out later." So we wrote on the blackboard above the bar, "Piggy and Yuk owe loads of bucks and Diesel Jack is coming and he is gay!" Oh, he wasn't by the way, we were just being daft!!

The next day we are down at the harbour and we have some lunch then takes a look around all these posh yachts. Piggy spots one of these beauties for sale and says to me, "Go and ask that fella over there how much they want for it." This guy looks all posh and tanned, blond hair, immaculate white shirt on. It turns out this lad is from Manchester.

He says, "I am here selling for my client, it's not my yacht," and he asks what we are up to. So we tell him we have been skiing and are now here for Grand Prix... and that we are going into town.

"Do you want to come with us?" we asked, 'cos he is clearly on his own.

That night we goes to pick him up. Well, he is all dressed up, white trousers, white silk shirt, white plimmies, blond hair, diamonds and jewellery and smelt very nice! So he jumps in the back of Piggy's truck and we head down into town. Now, whatever Piggy had done, this guy and done more of! If Piggy's cat was black, his was blacker! We 'ad a right one here!

We pull up outside Flashman's Bar, well... you couldn't move for people all over the pavement! Turns out, all the gays in Monte Carlo (called Monegasque Gays apparently!) had turned up looking for Diesel Jack! They all thought we were poofters arriving and this lad was Diesel! We never saw the lad again!!!!

We went in and says to Steve that we need to sort the tab out and he says, "Forget it lads! I have never had such a good two hours of business! All of Monaco's gays have been in my bar tonight because of your scribblings on the blackboard!"

Then we watched the Grand Prix before heading off for...

Bruges

So we are finally heading for home now. We got through Germany without too much hassle and we arrive in Bruges. We find a nice square to sit out in the early evening. Piggy asks me, "How much money have we got?"

I says, "We've got loads. German marks, French franks, Italian lira, Belgian bucks — about £700 worth in total."

This was all before the days of the Euro, of course.

Piggy had already got a bottle of expensive wine which turned out to be more than £100! So already, I was off to the Exchange Bureau to change this lot in to Belgian bucks. We decided (well Piggy did!) that we were stopping the night here even though we were close to getting home at this point. It had been three weeks now!

So I said to Piggy I would go and find a hotel for us to stop in. I went off and found one and got us booked in. Then I went and got into the Jeep which was parked in a car park somewhere near the square and I drove round the square to this hotel and went down underneath the hotel into its car park. I backed it up to this wall, got the suitcases out and took them up to hotel reception on one of the hotel trollies. A couple of lads then stepped forward 'cos I was struggling like hell with all this baggage of mine and Piggy's and gave me a hand to get it all upstairs to our room.

I get changed in to my tux, goes down to the bar and Piggy was already settled in for the night and was going nowhere!

I says, "Come on Piggy, let's go and explore," but no, he was stopping there. So off I go to have a look round. I find this bar with a load of English lads outside who turned out to be British soldiers. Well, they were taking the piss out of me with my white tux on, so I goes into the bar like James Bond and buys a drink and joins them.

I said, "Now, which of you buggers was gobbing off about my tux?"

Well, that broke the ice and we had a right good time! Course, I end up staying far too long supping with this lot and I suddenly realise I needed to get back and it is a bloody long walk! Now, in Bruges, there are a lot of push bikes around so I thought I would borrow one to get me back. Trouble was these cobble streets take a bit of negotiating with especially when you've got your tux on and had a van load of beer!

Even worse, these left hand drive bikes send you to the wrong side of the road and as I came round this bend wobbling away out of control, I crashes into a load of pedestrians walking across the road! Next minute, I am on the floor in my white jacket rolling about and making a right old mess of my smart tux!

So, I get back to the hotel and it's late by now and Piggy has finally left the bar and is tucked up in bed.

Next morning we wake up and Piggy says, "Right, we are going to go today. We need to get home now."

I says, "Yeah I know, I want to get back myself! Your pigs are busy pissing and shitting and going to market whereas my rally spares have been rusting away for the last three weeks!"

Piggy gets up and looks around for minute then says, "Where are the passports and all the money?"

"Haven't a clue!" I said. So, we empty out all our suitcases. Couldn't find them!

"Well, how much money have you got left?" says Piggy, "Do you have any brass left from last night?"

"About three francs!" says I.

"But you took about seven hundred with you when you left me!"

I searched through my pockets and a bit of shrapnel fell out but nothing else.

"Anyway, more to the point, where are the passports?"

Everything was missing: cash, passports, driving licences – the lot!

This was serious. We were stuck in a foreign country, no passports, no money!

So I says, "Don't worry mate, the Police station is next door". So I goes wobbling off into the Police station and I explain I have lost everything! Well, he had a pile of passports on his table! A huge heap of them! He starts going through them but nothing there! "Come back in an hour and we will take your details".

I walk back to the hotel and up to our room, but now there was no Piggy! I search around the room again and go through my torn tux and what do I find? Two hundred in the front pocket of my trousers, three hundred in my back pocket! Clever bugger me had split the money in case I got turned over and remembered I had given the rest to Piggy! What a relief!

I go downstairs and says to the bar man, "Where is he?"

"I think he is across the road" and sure enough there he is, sat in bar across square with our passports on the table!

"Where did you find these?" I asked.

"Under the back wheel of the Jeep in the car park!"

They must have dropped out when I dragged the bags out of the back of the Jeep! What a relief!

Finally, we arrive at the ferry, "Oh you are a day late!" says the woman taking the tickets!

"A day late?" I says to Piggy. The bugger had planned all along to be three weeks but he never bothered telling me!

61 – Daft names

I seem to accumulate a lot of daft names for various folk over the years, whether they are navigators or service crew. It's caused all sorts of problems too when I have booked tickets for ferries or rooms in hotels and they would say, full name and addresses, please! All I can say is, "Haven't a clue!" I had no idea who they were or where they lived!

"Well, there should be a room for Shitty Jim, Golly, Wardrobe and don't forget Codpiece and Billy Ballcock!"

Here are some of the names that come to mind. I have tried to remember their proper names, but have not entirely succeeded!

Nickname	Real name
Amos	Andy Moss
Animal	Steve Wilson
Bill Haley	Steve McNulty
Billy Ballcock	Dave Elcock
Billy Split Pin	Kevin Bardon
Bilko	Mike Jackson

Booler	Derek Parling
Bottles	Pete Stansfield (*Yorks Rally Spares, always worn brilliant bottle bottom glasses!*)
Chicken/Rocket/Sus/Lamby	Sue Lamb (*my ex-partner*)
Codpiece	Tony Coatsworth
Diesel Jack	John Machin (RIP)
Dudley Dave	No idea!
Fatty Jeff	No idea!
Eddie Goonderton	Eddie Ganderton
Gingespeed	Nigel Cay
Golly	Robin.....*nah, don't know but have known him years!*
Guernsey Tom	Tom Riordan
Half a Brain	Mick Dent
Handbag	Andrew Henrey
Huddersfield Chris	Chris Walker
Husky	Neil Hutchinson
Irish Pete	Pete Kitching
Joe Ninety	Richard Nightingale
Lubo	Bill Lumb
Mucky Bob	Rob Nowell (RIP)
Old Ianfield	Ian Oldfield
Pedal box Kev or Kevlar Kev	Kev Thompson
Piggy	David Thompson (RIP)
Pippa	Philippa......... *team coordinator*
Poncho	Pete McNeil
Queer Ken	Ken Hartley *wasn't queer I don't think!*
Raybog	Tony Raylor
Rocket	Sue Lamb

Rupert	John Close (RIP)
Shitty Jim	*No idea!*
Skids	Mark Skinner
Spinky	Richard Spink
Spug	Duncan Stead
Super Mick	Mick Penrose
Tall Paul	Paul Whitehead
Tiddles	Pete Fidell
Wan king	Martin King
Wardrobe	Ian Jemison
Wiggy	Errr... somebody Wigham
Wilf	Brian Pickles
Willybobs	Adrian Wilson
Wriggy /Wrigsby	Alan Wrigglesworth

Golly

Golly worked for this engineering company, machining and what have you. One day he was sat on his bench having his snap and his boss says to him, "You look like a gargoyle on the side of York Minster!", so the lads at his works started calling him "Gargoyle".

Anyway he starts getting interested in rallying and comes round to my place regularly.

I says to him, "What's your name?"

He says, "Robin, but everyone calls me Gargoyle." Anyway, I don't really know why but I ended up calling him Golly the Gargoyle and Golly stuck!"

There are loads more names but I am buggered if I can remember them!!!! Sorry anyone I have forgotten!

62 – Diesel Jack in Monte Carlo

Diesel Jack (real name John Machin – RIP) had nowt to do with rallying he was just a bit mad! He was a good pal of mine and Piggy's and had that ability to turn up when you least expected him to! He got into all sorts of scrapes! He was very much like an untameable Fred Dibnah! Diesel would have made a brilliant TV documentary if you could just calm him down!

He and his brother were one of the biggest sheep buyers in the UK. They would buy these sheep and export them to Italy and France and had a fleet of triple layer container wagons to ferry the sheep in. They would buy the sheep at the market, take them home to their lovely farm in North Yorkshire, fatten them up for a bit then whistle them off to Europe.

A law came in which stipulated that the animal had to be have a 'lairage'. This is a stopover point to water and feed them and give them exercise. Diesel bought a farmstead in France to make into a lairage, so he would often be in France.

One year me and Piggy were at the Monaco Grand Prix and we were in Rosie's Cafe. I had gone to the gents' and when I came back, Piggy says, "You will never guess who's here – Diesel!" He had come down from the lairage with his Aussie mate in all his mucky jeans with sheep shit all over his boots and here he is in middle of Monte Carlo!

He had booked into this fancy hotel next to Flashman's, so we head up there to see our old mate Steve who runs the bar. We had a few in there and then on to a posh restaurant Piggy had booked for lunch at Casino Square for practice and race day. This was an ideal place to go 'cos it had a balcony on the first floor where you can watch the race from.

We were sat on this balcony watching practice and I had these Yukspeed stickers which Oz had stuck all over his jumper and then they were getting stuck onto anyone else going past! Diesel sees this posh looking Chinese lady and decides to plant one firmly on her bum! Well, this doesn't go down at all well... she turns round... and her husband starts Kung Fooing! Diesel starts talking in Italian 'cos he looked like he could come from Italy... I looks at Piggy and says, "let's fuck off; he can look after himself!" and leave Diesel to calm things down on his own!

Later on, we meet up again in another posh hotel near the harbour. There is Oz wandering about still with his jumper covered in Yukspeed stickers and we are searching around trying to find Diesel. I try to get Oz smartened up... "take your jumper off Oz," which he does, then turns it inside out and puts it back on!!!

We are walking through this lovely hotel and I see Diesel, "Oz, they are over here!" With that, Oz walks through the door as everyone looks at him and he trips and flies across the floor! Oh dear, more embarrassment!

Finally, we move on again to the famous Rosie's Bar. Practice had finished by now. We had consumed so much drink by this time, but we decided it is time for gin and tonics. We are stood outside on the pavement having a drink, and inside there are these Germans having a meal. There are glass sliding doors on to pavement outside Rosie's Bar. I says to Diesel, "Hey, you be careful, don't lean on that patio door; you'll go through it!"

"What door?" he says leaning across, but the door was open and he goes flying through it and lands on this German's table... food and drink goes flying everywhere! Oh, the embarrassment again! My throat hurt with laughing! It cost poor old Diesel a fortune to pay off the Germans and put things right!

Finally, we decides it is time to get back to the hotel and Diesel says he will take us and goes and collects his Volvo estate car... poor old Oz is paralytic!

"Piggy," I says, "we are going to struggle to get Oz into the car 'cos his legs have fallen off! We've got to get him up these steps, along a footpath, over the Armco and into Diesel's estate car!"

Piggy says, "Why?"

I says, "I'm fuckin' legless as well!"

Piggy says, "I'm not much better myself, but we will give it a go!"

Anyway we got him up and in through the tailgate of the estate car, but we had to leave the tailgate up 'cos we couldn't get him any further inside and off we drove! How we got away with that I just do not know!

So, how did you get the name Yuk?

Yorkshire Evening Press (formerly the local York evening paper now the York Press): "Nicknamed Yuk, a title that has something to do with his deep throated laughter ..."

63 – Yuk gets the jewel

I got my first Millington engine in 1991. I had not particularly enjoyed the G3s even though I did have some success with them. I decided to go back to a Mk. 2.

This is how Motoring News explained the change:

> *"Yuk gets the jewel."*
>
> *"Yuk Hodgson, Yorkshire wit and wheeler dealer, has finally laid his hands on a Millington Diamond engine after six months of searching.*
>
> *He has bought Martin Thomas's Escort and plans to install the engine in a virtually unused 16 year old Mk. 2 Escort shell in time for the next round of the BTRDA Gold Star Championship, the Quinton Stages Rally. Hodgson is delighted with the car and plans to register it with the ex-works number plate from his Mk. 3 rear wheel drive Escort. It will be the first time he has so much as driven using an engine with the power of the latest Millington engine.*
>
> *He also has to pay for the Diamond motor. However, that shouldn't present much of a problem now that he has the remains of Thomas's Escort for sale."*

Buying the Millington engine really worked out well. Martin Thomas from Wales had bent his car and wanted rid. It had quite a famous 'POO 491R' registration with the car too. I went down to see him and I asked what he was going to do next. He said he was thinking of moving over to Gp. N with a Galant. It just so happened Piggy had been rallying his ex-Pentti Airikkala championship winning car and was ready to sell it, so Martin bought the complete package from Piggy! Amazing timing!

One of the most memorable rallies I did in the Millington was when it was new. I entered the Lakeland Rally with Crofty. There was loads of snow on the tops and Petchy (Steve Petch) was doing the rally in his Gp.N Cossy. Young Alistair McRae was in that red and yellow prize drive Shell Sapphire. He won the rally but we finished 2nd which was such a great result!

We got to the bar at the finish and the organiser says, "We have got to give you a bollocking!"

"What for?" I says,

"You've been putting petrol in your car"

"I know I need to get round the rally, like!"

"Yeah, but you did it in the service area and there was a designated area for refuelling."

"Oh was there? I've been doing the same thing for years."

"Well, some of the other organisers are saying we should give you a 30 minute penalty, but I turned round and told them you're going to have to get rid of the top six if that is the case, so we knocked that on head!"

I says, "Is that me bollocked then?"

He says, "Yes."

So I said, "Ok then, get me a whisky in!"

Later that year, we were doing one of the rounds up in Kielder and we were seeded behind the late Willie Rutherford in his Mazda rotary engined thing. He never turned the thing off and by it was a noisy, smoky thing with a big cone chimney poking out of the back! It was bloody well stinking me out! What a noisy bastard thing it was, "Willie, will you turn that fuckin thing off?!!!"

"And you can fuck off an' all, Yuk!" and he left it turned on!

I did two full BTRDA seasons with that Millington car with Crofty and one or two other events including the Bushwacker in Ireland. By, that car did work well, but towards the end of the year the recession was catching up on us all and I decided to pack it in. Well, Rally Sport magazine got wind of this (I think through Mark Lowe) and they came down and took some pictures of me and the car just up the road near Castle Howard and Simon Cooke interviewed me. They did a right nice four page spread and headlined it *"Endangered Species"* in the December 1992 edition:

> *"Every sport needs its characters. Football has Gazza, snooker Hurricane*
> *Higgins and tennis John McEnroe. Rallying is in grave danger of losing one of*
> *its most colourful characters, Yorkshire's larger than life Yuk Hodgson.*

Yuk, a regular competitor in the Gold Star and Clubman's championships and a member of Yorkshire's rallying mafia, has his faithful Escort up for sale and looks destined to retire at the end of the year, another victim of the recession.

"It's a vicious circle,", he explains in his broad Yorkshire accent. "I need other people to be buying parts from me so that I can afford to go rallying myself, and there just aren't enough customers around at the moment.

.......'"you have to draw the line somewhere and decide enough is enough, and I am at that stage now." Hence the 'for sale' sign notice on his much loved Escort."

I sold the shell to Craig McIntosh in the end.

Billy Split Pin (Kevin Bardon)

64 – My first ever rally... and it was with Yuk!

Yuk and I built this Mk. 2 with the Millington in it (GJN) in two months and two days. I would come down to his workshop every night (5.30pm to 11.00pm) and every weekend. Yuk would work on it during the day when not selling to customers. The car was originally going to have a BD fitted but we put two tunnels in it so we could fit a Millington if we could find one. Fortunately, the Millington came up at the last minute by buying Martin Thomas's car in Wales with a famous "POO" registration. All we wanted was the engine but Yuk bought the whole car damaged including a van full of spares which he could then sell on.

Billy Split Pins first ever rally!

The shell for GJN came off Yuk's forecourt. It was a really nice complete flat front RS2000 road car. We stripped it down to a bare shell and built it from the ground up.

We had two very successful years with that car doing the full BTRDA championship and other rallies too including events abroad. Out of 22 rallies in that car, I think we had something like two retirements and I serviced on most of those events for Yuk and Peter Croft. It was the first rally car I had ever built and I learnt lots doing it.

To say thank you for helping him build the car, I was offered the chance to do a single venue rally with Yuk on an old World War 2 airfield near York called Melbourne. We had been to Wales on the Saturday to do the Cambrian with Crofty and Yuk said if they finished that event in one piece and we got home in time we would ring the organisers and see if we could get a run. We got home safely, Yuk rang the organisers up and yes we could have an entry seeded at six. You could say it was in at the deep end for me, but Crofty said he would come along and look after me to make sure I didn't make any mistakes.

Of course, what happens on a rally is Yuk has so many friends who want to talk to him, we were slow getting down to the first stage as he kept talking to every Tom, Dick and Harry and we end up being delayed and book in a minute late! We then had lost a minute in stage times already and we had not even started a stage! My first ever rally, my first ever time control and I clocked in a minute late! I was clueless, no idea what was going on!

There were eight stages in total and over the first six we clawed back 58 seconds and were second overall to Ian Tiffany, a local lad in a Sunbeam also with a Millington fitted. Then it got dark. Yuk, as we all know does not like the dark one bit. At one point I had to say to him, "Do you mind driving at t' other side of the road, we are on the wrong side of the cones!" as we hurtled down the main runway!

If the stages had remained in daylight, I think we could have won quite easily, but not when it got dark. We finished second overall about sixteen seconds behind Ian Tiffany in the end, losing time over the last two stages. It was still a great result though and I was hooked!

So, how did you get the name Yuk?

Someone once said, "Peter 'Yuk' Hodgson … His real name is Yuk really but Peter is his Sunday name!"

Billy Split Pin (Kevin Bardon)
65 – Drinking with The Yorkshire Mafia

In the early nineties, The Yorkshire Mafia (often talked about in the weekly motoring magazines) consisted of Yuk, Steve Bannister, of course, Vince Chapman, Jeff McNeil, Warren Philliskirk and Andy Elliott mainly. They were all doing the BTRDA championship. Yuk and Vince had Millington engined Mk. 2s, Jeff's and Steve's Mk. 2s were BDAs, Warren had a Mk. 2 with the Wilcox built naturally aspirated Cosworth and Andy was using his ex-Alex Jackson red Opel Manta 400.

They were all competitive in the stages and we usually met up at the finish for a few drinks. I think it was in 1991 that the Hadrian Centurion Rally was based at the Novotel at Newcastle Airport.

At the finish Yuk says, "Are we going home or are we having a couple of pints first?" Well, I couldn't drink because I knew I was driving the barge home with the rally car on the back and I also knew once he started drinking there was no going home! On this particular event, I was really knackered. We had driven up very early that morning and I wanted to get home to bed; it had been a long day.

It got to nine or ten o'clock and I says to him, "Yuk, I need to get home now."

"No, no, come on, the party is just starting. I'm going to have a few more!"

"Alright then," I said, "I am off home."

I called his bluff a couple of times, but no, he wasn't moving so I thought "bollocks, I am going". I got in the van and set off without him! Apparently he did come running out and tried to catch up with me. I never saw him and left him behind! I knew he would get a lift from someone else easily the next day but I'd had enough!

Anyway, that worked because any time I said I was on my way home after that incident, he came with me!

66 – Seizoen shenanigans

We did the Seizoen Rally in Belgium in the Millington as well, in 1992, I think.

The rally was sponsored by the Seizoen Brewery. Just before we set off, one of the service lads let me down right at the last minute and just didn't turn up. Poor old

Billy Split Pin had to service on his own. He had to read the map himself and drive and find the end of each stage on his own. But he was there every time, what a star! We finished 9th overall.

At the finish there was a marquee in the market square and we all walked in. I introduced myself to this nice lady and said, "Do you mind if I bring my friends in?" These were Crofty, Billy Split Pin and David Bell's team were there too. We all go in and all they had was this Seizoen's beer. They came in lovely glasses but after a few of them you get fed up and I fancied something else!

So I goes over to this lovely lady again and says, "It is really nice that you invited us over here and that you have closed public roads over here." I asked her, "How do you get your road closures so easy?"

She says, "Well, my husband is the Chief Constable and is also the Managing Director of Seizoen's brewery... oh, and he is also the secretary of the rally! So he just says right we are going to close this road for the rally and it happens!!"

Then I ask her if she has any other drinks. "Oh, just a moment," she replied and she goes into this fridge under the table and brings out what looks like a bottle of bitter lemon.

Well, all the locals stood to one side and took a big intake of breath! I only get a little drop and I says to Crofty, "Just try that. What do you think?"

"Mmm, very nice," says Crofty,

"Right," I said, "fill her up to the top, my drink taster thinks it's ok!"

After few of these, I get fed up of it, so we go back to the beer again. Then I remembered I had a bottle of whisky in the barge! So I went and got a bottle of whisky out, filled the lads glasses up with whisky... then we thought we would have some more beer... then yet more lemon juice!

Well, after midnight, following the presentation, I decided to go to the toilet outside. As soon as I get outside, my legs went from under me!!

I was only about hundred yards away but I knew I couldn't go any further so I found a bench and thought I would lie on that. Then it occurred to me, they will think I have gone home and they probably wouldn't find me! Finally, I headed for my road car (a Mercedes estate car) and soon as I got to it I collapsed on the ground!

Eventually, some of the locals come out of the tent and say,

"He's here, he's here!"

They then pick me up and try pushing me in to the front of the car not realising it was right hand drive and they were trying to get me behind the steering wheel!

We got all this on the camcorder so I have the proof!

About a year later, Tony Raylor invited me over to Harrogate to help on some classic rally and I got introduced to this Belgian bloke who shakes my hand and says he has met me in his home country and explains that saw me on the pavement later after a heavy night's drinking!

"What was in that lemon juice drink?" I asked,

"Poteen," he says; "hundred per cent proof!"

No wonder I couldn't keep on my feet!

Billy Split Pin (Kevin Bardon)
67 – Yuk goes rallycrossing

We took the Mk. 2 Millington (GJN) up to Middlesbrough to do his one and only rallycross event at Langbaurgh, Teesside. He was in the rally car class and was brilliant to watch, treating the crowds to huge power slides around the circuit. He started to run out of tyres though. The car was so powerful and he was giving it large and laying down so much rubber on the tarmac!

At the end he was all for loading the car up and going home. He wasn't bothered. Announcements were coming over the Tannoy saying he was now in the finals too which he was not ready for! Anyway, he won so many trophies that day we needed a wheelbarrow to take them home! He won the Rally Car class, he got FTD (Fastest Time of the Day) which got him in to the finals and he finished something like sixth or seventh overall, plus an award for "Entertainer of the Day". What a classic day!

68 – The offensive cell phone incident

It would be around 1991. We were sat in a pub the night before the Silva Stages. Kevin Furber was one of those up and coming young bucks in the Peugeot team and he came up to me with a fancy new mobile phone (it was that era!).

Well, it was a fuckin' huge cell phone! "Oh, mint is this thing!" says Kevin – big as a fuckin' brick it was! Then he wrote something on the screen saying, "Yuk is a c..nt," or something like that!

"By that's clever is that Kevin, i'nt it?"

"Yeah," he says, but I was feeling a bit pissed off with what he had written on it.

"Oh it does everything!" he says.

"Is it water proof?" I says.

"Oh aye!"... so I put it in a pint of cider!

It didn't work after that! He took it all to bits, puffing and blowing into it.

"Give it to me," I said. "I will take it to Gavin at TV Centre in Malton. He'll fix it."

I took it to Gavin's and Gavin says, "It's fucked!"

Well, Kevin got his solicitors after me so I had to defend myself. I says, "Look don't waste your money. You'll get nowt off me. He wrote some quite profound obscenities on the screen about me which I was not too happy about," and that was all that was said.

I felt a bit sorry for Kevin 'cos it cost about seven hundred quid in them days and he needed it for his business; I still have it in a drawer somewhere!

69 – Lost in Jersey with Handbag!

I have known Handbag (Andrew Henrey) for quite a few years. He is a Guernsey lad. He has been buying bits off me for a long time. A lot of Jersey and Guernsey lads rally Escorts. He rings me up one day and says, "Yuk, will you come over and drive my car?"

I says, "Why, what's up?"

He says, "Oh, I lost my licence for 28 days 'cos I was caught speeding and I have entered the Jersey Rally and I don't want to miss it!"

He had this Pinto engined Escort, Rocket box with an English axle. He says, "Bring your seat over and we can put it in and get it all set up for you."

I flew over there and he picked me up and put me in a hotel which was great. When I get to see the car – well, I have not done so much work on a car in a week as I have on my own cars in a year!

No screen washers!

"We don't need them!" he says,

I says, "We do need them!"

I had the LSD out of the axle; I had the steering rack off; I know I had the pedal box out; lots of things needed sorting out. I was knackered!

Eventually, I says, "I am off back to the hotel for a shower and a lie down!" and he carried on finishing the car off!

Anyway, come the rally, I don't think he had done much co-driving. I had never driven a Pinto before, but I was finding my feet. We had one spin on a square right and lodged it between two banks so had to do a load of shunting backwards and forwards about twenty times to get sorted, but then it starts to come together. Well, he's waving at his mates, his legs are going all over place, he's waving his fuckin' arms about!

I says, "Andy, will you sit still!!!" It was so distracting! Next, I come to this one corner and I handbrake it round and it comes round mint; well, he starts yelping and clapping!

"Andy, will you fuckin' sit still!!!!!!"

He is jumping up and down waving to folks and having a right good time, but I just couldn't concentrate!!!

We had done one service and we had to do another loop then back to St Helier. Well, could we find service? Could we hellers!!! We were up this street then down another. I says, "Andy, for fuck's sake, what's going on?"

"I don't know Yuk, stop here, stop here!"

He is completely lost, bits of paper and maps all over the place!!!! We are really starting to run out of time now.

He jumps out to ask some folks... jumps back in the car... "right turn round..."

"Andy, I've got some news for you, I can't turn round – it's a one way street!" We end up stopping and asking other folks... no, still lost.

"Leave it to me," I says.

We pulls up beside this young lad stood outside a chip shop.

"Excuse me fella," as he is eating his chips, "do you know where service is?"

"Aye, I know!"

"Do you mind jumping in and showing us?"

Poor old Andy has to get in the back around the roll cage, intercom and all that stuff! Luckily, he is a skinny youth! So we have this little Jonny sat in the front with his chips, loving his ride in a rally car and sure enough he gets us there!

"Thank you very much," I says, after eating half his chips!

We finally get booked into service, but we are ever so late.

One of top lads on Jersey (Chris Le Bonniec) asks how we are doing and I tell him.

He said, "Oh, they might let you off," but no, we go OTL (Over Time Limit) and we had to pull out.

I said to Andy, "Andy, I have come all this way, spent nearly a week building your fuckin' car and then you get us lost and out of time; you had better get all the beer in!!!"

It were mint! I really enjoyed myself and I really appreciated Andy asking me to drive his car; it was a privilege and we did laugh!

I had never rallied in Jersey before, it was my first time and I fancied going back at some point.

70 – Yuk goes BMW

I bought the Prodrive-built M3 from John Price. He had used it on the Manx a couple of times. A lot of people thought I bought the one from Peter Lloyd which was advertised as the ex-Brian Bell car, but that didn't come off, so I went to see John Price and did a deal with him. Graham Middleton had originally bought it but hardly used it. I think Mike Rimmer had it before Pricey got it.

It was quick and lovely to drive. About 295 bhp and a dog box. So much faster than an Escort. Piggy says, "It'll take you a thousand stage miles to get used to it!"

It was left hand drive and I couldn't get on with that so converted it to right hand drive, which was a doddle. It was a lovely car.

I had a few moments with it mind!

Me and Crofty did Charlemagne two years running. First year we did really, really well; First British finisher, I think it was. At the finish we were invited up to the podium to get our awards which we did, then we came down and went to the back... then they wanted us back on to the podium again and they started playing 'We are the Champions'.

It was a brilliant result in the new car, sixteenth overall and first British crew.

In 1994 I did the Crystal Stages with John Birkett. Everyone had gone Gp. N Cossy, but we went M3 instead. The scrutineers at that time were keen to make sure people were not using oversized restrictors on the Cossy Escorts. We had a bit of a hold up at the stage start and we were just milling around having a natter. Jim, the scrutineer, was going round all the cars checking the restrictor plates on the turbos. He gets to Ian Joel's car and puts his calliper in to measure it... pulls it out... alters it a bit more... it still doesn't touch the sides!

Poor old Jim couldn't see very well but says, "Well that's a lot more than 94 millimetres! I think you have a problem here."

"Why what's up?"

He says, "Well my calliper won't touch the sides of your restrictor plate."

"Oh, well it was alright when we set off! What do we do now?" says Ian.

Jim says, "We report it to the stewards, you carry on."

At the finish, we were mocking a few of these Cossy owners who had got caught out for having illegal restrictors in. Anyway, those that were cheating all got fined and banned for six months! I loved that quote though... "Well, it was alright when we left!"

Crofty and I did Donegal in the M3 and I was having problems with my ears! There was some stuff in my ears and they were all watery. Once I pulled my helmet on I couldn't hear a thing! I was all out of balance!

The first three stages on Friday, Crofty is blathering away on the notes like and shouts, "Square right at bungalow," but I don't hear a thing and shoot straight off the road across someone's grass into the bloody hedge!

He was still blathering on with notes and I have to say, "Hang on Crofty," 'till we get off this women's hedge and back on the road!

So, we get into service and I asked Booler (Derek Parling) if we'd got some screen washer pipe. We send a load of mineral water down the pipe to clear me lug hole! Anyway that doesn't do any good so I decided I need a doctor and get off to Derry hospital. Elvis, one of my loyal service crew, takes me down and this doctor gets a machine and sucks all this debris out; it worked a treat!

Next day the earth lead falls off and we retire to the pub for a load of Smithwicks. The following day we get towed back but we have to stop at every pub on the way! The trailer is still at Letterkenny so we are on a rope. We stops at one pub and after Elvis gets in my old Mercedes estate car (which was my barge then), he sets off not knowing that Jeff McNeil had unhooked the bloody race car from the Merc! Elvis set off and goes about a hundred yards before he realises!! Elvis didn't half curse!!! We laughed all the way home!

Billy Split Pin (Kevin Bardon)
71 – The new BMW arrives at Barton Hill

I was down at his house at Barton Hill the day Yuk arrived home with the BMW on the trailer. We got the car off the trailer and Yuk says, "Let's go for a ride and try it out."

Now this car was left hand drive. We set off out of his road and headed up towards Castle Howard. It felt lovely, just trying out the power, going steady around the bends then giving it some big licks along the long straight on the Castle Howard estate and up the hill through the two arches on the straight road heading up towards the big house.

At the top, we turned around and headed back down again, back through the two arches again then Yuk says, "Let's see how she flies!" He nailed it going back down the hill to a big crest on the long straight and we gets in to 5th gear, hit the crest and flew........ and landed on the grass verge on the left hand side of the road! We nearly binned it! He looked at me and pulled a face and we headed home not quite as fast!

As he put the car in to the garage he says to me, "That is the last time I drive a left hand drive rally car!"

And it was.

72 – Jim Kitson and the mustard incident

Me and Jim Kitson were doing Donegal and while we were making pace notes, we stopped at a shop to get some sandwiches. Anyway, a bit further down the road we parked up next to a loch side and get out the ham, butter and bread, a bit of salad and a tube of mustard. I make up my sandwich and it was all very nice.

Anyway, we set off and carry on recceing. Later in the day we stop for another sandwich and I couldn't find the mustard! "Where's the mustard Jim?"

"I put it on the roof of car!"

"Right, OK Jim, so we will have it without mustard shall we?" I wasn't happy at all!!

We came back and did the same route again we had done in the morning and what's on the tarmac but a squashed tube and a big squirt of mustard right across road?!!! So he got a bollocking for that 'cos I like a bit of mustard on my sandwiches!!!

Billy Split Pin (Kevin Bardon)
73 – Kall Kwik in the BMW M3

I was really looking forward to co-driving for Yuk on the Kall Kwik Rally in the BMW in February 1995. On the Thursday night before the rally, I got a phone call from Yuk saying, "Billy, I've done my back in, but don't worry I've got a driver sorted out. Come down tomorrow night and you can meet him."

At that point I had only done about three rallies so I still had lots to learn. The next night I am down at Yuk's workshop getting the spares sorted out for the service barge and I had my head down getting some stuff from under the bench when I heard the clicking of posh brogue shoes on the garage floor... I turned around... and it is the one and only Mr. Piggy Thompson! Ok, I thought, no pressure!

So Piggy sat in the car to check the seat positioning and says, "yeah, that will do fine."

Yuk said, "Do you want a drive in it, Piggy?"

"No, it will be fine". He had never been in the car before.

The next morning, the rally started from Eden Camp war museum just outside Malton. It was really cold, icy and a bit snowy in places, the usual February weather in Yorkshire. We set off from his house and drove the car up to the start to get a feel for it.

First stage was up the road past Pickering and I was looking for the Cayley Arms on the A170 to turn left up into the forests. Somehow, we missed the turning and soon after I realised I had missed something. I said, "Whoa, something is wrong, Piggy!"

"Don't worry, you'll sort it out," said Piggy as calm as anything. We turned round and he says to me, "Right, that is just a mistake, don't worry about it," and we took the correct turning up into the forests. As we made our way up into the stage, he tells me to tighten my belts and he gave the car a good old blast up the forest road up to the stage; what a car, it had some serious grunt!

The differences between Yuk's driving style and Piggy's driving style in the same car were like night and day. Yuk would usually set the car up using the handbrake but Piggy used more of a Finnish style, using the Scandinavian flick before each bend and rarely used the handbrake at all, maybe half a dozen times in the whole event. He would just set the car up before the bend, sideways before it but straight coming out and then gone; we were on maps then, no notes, of course.

One of the most memorable moments was going up Spires straight in Cropton Forest on sheet ice. When I looked up from the maps, the road was white as white can be. Piggy said to me, "This is where the old boys make time up."

I said, "It's straight, straight, straight all the way up to the top".

He went up the box right up to 6th without hesitation. That BMW made a really distinctive noise when 6th was selected.

I couldn't help wonder how he was going to make it stop at the end of this long straight, going into the hairpin on this slippery ice. We stormed up that hill, then the next minute we were on the left hand side gulley in the grass and loose stones bringing the speed down, no problem at all!

We got some results shoved through the window at half way and he says to me, "I'm not worried about results, I am only out for a play." We were 8th overall in amongst all these four wheel drive Cossies.

Piggy said, "I am driving like a Granny today."

So I just said, "We're doing very well, let's just carry on as we are."

I thought to myself, what is he going to be like when he is driving properly?

So, we carried on and, of course, in those days without the really quick computerised results we get today, we didn't know how we were progressing apart from that update at halfway. We finished a remarkable 3rd overall! Neil Hiorns won it in his 4 w/d Cossy and Martin Rowe was 2nd in his works Peugeot Maxi.

I remember us finishing and having a bottle of champagne at the end! It was such a great opportunity to go with Piggy. He was such a legend. My very first rally was with the legendary Yuk Hodgson and on only my fourth event now with the legendary Piggy Thompson; that is something really special!

Paul Skinner
74 – Bare-breasted Indian beauties!

My first event with Yuk co-driving for him was The Des Winks Stages on Wombleton Airfield in 1995. It was in the BMW and we were seeded about car 3.

At the start, there was the usual banter with fellow competitors, marshals etc. and as we pull up to the start line Yuk reaches under his seat and pulls out an Indian language newspaper! The night before he'd been in Malton at the Indian restaurant where he'd picked it up! It was the equivalent of The Sun complete with topless centre spread. So at the start line Yuk is reading the paper and gives the marshals a good giggle.

I found out by accident how to annoy Yuk! As on all rallies, at the start I was a little nervous and as a consequence my stomach was a little upset and it would manifest itself in ever so small little burps. These were amplified somewhat by the intercom and Yuk would get really pissed off at me!!! Once we started I was fine, but on the start line for stage one he was muttering and chuntering at me!!!

We ran pretty well until the 4th or 5th stage when one of the (according to Yuk) bullet proof half shafts let go big style!! Rather than trudge back to the service area we decided to wait for the tow at the stage end and Yuk settled down to spectate on the errant wheel and half shaft. He placed himself right on the braking point to a big square chicane and proceeded to cheer everyone on and just as they entered the braking zone, he'd leap a couple of feet forward and open the newspaper to the page with the bare breasted Indian beauties! I can't tell you how many completely missed their braking point!!

As always – hilarious!!

Paul Skinner
75 – No fat bewers!

I think it was the Cadwell Stages Rally in 1997. -we were seeded at one, as Yuk had won it the previous year and we were in the BMW again.

The format of the event had changed with night stages being introduced and so we had the service van with the rally car on the trailer and then Yuk's so called "motor home" which was in fact a 1970s caravan towed by another van loaded with stuff. We looked like the rallying version of the Clampetts (The Hillbillies)!!

When we arrive we are strategically set up as close to the clubhouse bar as you could possibly get and so to the event.

We were trading times in the top three until night fell, and on the first night stage we had a disaster. Never, and I mean NEVER go out at night with Yuk driving! He can't see past the end of his nose!! I'm calling out corners, features, arrows some of which we were virtually parked next to and he just couldn't see them! So, for the second night stage our plan is to slowly pull away from the start and park about 100 yards down the stage and wait for the car behind us to start and pull out right behind him and follow him home! That is exactly what we did!!!

Once we'd set up in the service area, we also set up a stand/display of 'Yukspeed/Barton Hill Racing and No Fat Bewers' sun visors available for purchase at a pound. It was self-service and you just put the spondulicks in the ashtray provided! These funds were drunk in the clubhouse nightly and loads more besides. For those of you wondering, 'bewers' is an impolite, non-PC word for girlfriends.

In 'the motor home', Yuk had fitted a larger toilet than the space provided could accommodate and as a consequence, you couldn't sit on it and close the door!! So I awoke from my alcoholic stupor on Sunday morning to see Yuk on the throne with pants around his ankles, reading some rally publication and smoking a fag. A sight so embedded on my brain that I'll remember it until the day I die!

After the night stages, we had dropped right out of contention but we slowly clawed our way back into the top 10 and we were so relaxed we even had a drink in the clubhouse at the lunch halt!

At this time, Yuk was off around service on his little Monkey bike, resplendent in his East German border guard hat with the fur ear muffs, a sort of Yorkshire version of Elmer Fudd! While he is away, this chap in a Barbour jacket, Hunter wellingtons and sporting a fine flat cap and clipboard comes up to me and asks if am selling the sun strips. I explained I was not the vendor and he went on to say he worked for MCD who owned the circuit and that you had to have a vendor's licence to sell such items and it cost only £80 for the weekend! I suggested he needed to see the chap in the funny hat, so off he goes. I just knew this would be too good to miss so I tagged along!

On finding Yuk, the MCD chap goes into a long and very convoluted reason as to why Yuk has to fork out £80 for this licence and Yuk just stands there not saying a word and totally expressionless. When finally this MCD chap has finished, Yuk takes a step towards him puts his nose about one inch from MCD chaps and says, "You know what you can do don't you?"

MCD says, "No."

Yuk replies. "Fook Right Off!!!"

This chap went as white as a sheet and scuttled off never to be seen or heard from again!

76 – The Rothmans coloured Mk. 2

I took a Mk. 2 Escort in the lovely Rothmans colour scheme in part exchange when I sold the BMW to Melvyn Evans from South Wales. It was not a bad little car with a right nice Millington in the front. I entered the Charlemagne Rally in France with Terry Wilson, a local lad from just up the road in Malton.

It has always been a problem getting a trolley jack under a Mk. 2 when on 13 inch wheels and fitted with racing tyres, so I got Roy Jarvis at Ralloy to make me some two inch ramps to drive the car onto, then the trolley jack would go under back axle nicely. We came in to service first time and the lads line up the ramps under my car. Next thing, the rear ramps shot out and nearly cuts the legs off a lad stood directly behind car! Poor lad! I learnt then that we needed to have studs in the bottom of the ramps to dig into tarmac!

Bill Lumb

77 – Donegal Yarns – Holding hands

It would be the height of all the troubles in Ireland in 1975/76. We took the Stranraer to Larne ferry crossing and we were on the quay at Larne and there was a delay for some reason or other. There were 45 gallon oil drums filled with cement used as 'sleeping soldiers'.

Dave Bullock from York was with us. He's was a butcher, good and strong. Whilst messing about, Dave went over and picked up one of these oil drums! It was incredible! I don't even know how he got it off the ground!

We then went on to Letterkenny to our hotel. There was such a big gang of us all from York Motor Club, about thirty five or thirty six people in all who Yuk had brought over. In the evening, we all met up at one of the pre-rally parties and we were stood in a big circle having a drink when this big Irish lad breaks through the circle and says, "Would anyone like to shake the hands of an Irishman?"

Everyone looked at each other and then looked at Dave Bullock. We thought if anyone is going to shake hands it can be Dave Bullock! So Dave moved in to the middle of the circle not really understanding what was going on. They squared up to each other, Dave still having no idea what was happening and this guy then starts shaking Dave's hand and then begins to squeeze even more... and then more... and you can see Dave's face looking in more and more pain as they looked at each other eye to eye! Dave starts to squeeze back now and by this time the whole of the floor is looking on and people are starting to chant and got louder and louder!

Eventually the Irish lad fell to his knees, tears in his eyes and gave up! The whole place erupted! This guy was apparently the local champion and Dave had got him!

78 – Donegal Yarns – Quick as a flash!

In the early seventies, we had Elvis (famous for his brilliant droopy moustache and his massive cigars) in the chase car. We had a young lass who came with us from York for the trip too. I won't say who she was – got to be discreet, eh?! As we pulled in behind the chase car at the side of the road, up comes her T shirt, out with her tits, like, then pulled it back down laughing her head off!

"Did you see that?" says Lubo in the co-driver's seat... old Elvis was slavering under his moustache and chewing on his ceeeegar!

Spectator control in Donegal

Mike Greasley
79 – Donegal Yarns – Young studs!

I remember once in Ireland the service crew of a non-starting Yorkshire pig farmer in a Porsche (enough of a clue?) for whom I was supposed to be co-driving, financed their trip by selling certain rubber items in the toilets to the rampant young studs; such goods were not readily available at the time. They made a fortune, having obtained a large stock from a local chemist's on the grounds that they were visitors to the area – something to do with improving Anglo-Irish relations.

Yuk had set up a table in the gents' loos in the Rally HQ hotel and was selling them by the dozens to anyone who wanted them!

Super Mick (Mick Penrose)
80 – Donegal Yarns – The beer fight!

We had some amazing times in Donegal in the seventies. Some people say, "If you can remember the sixties, you weren't there!" Well for us, it was the seventies in Donegal. If you can remember the Donegal Rallies in the seventies, you weren't there!

Our first visit to Donegal was chaos! We met the hotel manager Mr. McGarvey who was having a drink with us at the bar one night. We were having a lot of banter and Yuk ends up pouring his pint of bitter over this poor manager's head, even though he was in a very smart suit… so the manager pours his over Yuk… who orders more beer and the beer fight begins! Everyone is chucking drinks at each other, ice cubes were going down people's shirts; it was like a Mexican Wave as more people joined in – total chaos!

One night we were out and found a piss pot in the middle of the road! Bizarre, I know. Naturally, Yuk said, "We'll 'ave that!" and we took it back, washed it up of course, and then stuck a rally sticker on it and I used it as a hat! Don't know why! Anyway, I have photographs to prove it!

Animal (Steve Wilson)
81 – Donegal Yarns – Gin and milk

I remember very well him doing the gin and milk thing in Donegal one time when we went over to abuse our livers!

We'd had a fairly serious session and decided to go watching the next morning. So off we go, and the first village we get to his lordship shouts, "Stop we need some milk!!!" We didn't have a kettle so a brew was out of the question.

Anyway it was a typical Irish setup; front door, corridor, shop on the right and the bar on the left. He disappears into the shop for a moment then comes out taking the top off a pint of milk, into the bar and pours half the milk into a pint glass then says to the landlord/shopkeeper or whoever he was, "Just pop three gins in there, mate." If that isn't a champion's breakfast, I don't know what is!

82 – Donegal Yarns – Awards for everything!

We had such a mint time the first time in Donegal, I brought a huge party with me the next year! Twenty five to thirty folks from York came with us. It was brilliant! We had people like Lubo again, Jeff McNeil, Pip Dale, Ian Oldfield and loads and loads of other great people with us... we had such a great time; it was one big party!

You get an award for everything in Donegal, even just for turning up! Anyway, at the finish we got an award for bringing the most people!!!

That year they ran the event without pace notes to try and even things up and make it fair for everyone. Well, John Taylor had a huge accident on one bend and a few followed him in including Ian Oldfield! Boy, there was some carnage! I think they went back to pace notes after that!

Christine Oldfield
83 – Donegal Yarns – We did laugh!

Dave Bullock was trying to drink out of a milk bottle as he was sat in the back of Yuk's service barge as we drove along. Yuk spotted this and jammed on the brakes so milk came spilling out all over Dave's jumper... poor lad, it must have stunk after that!

One of the days, we went off spectating and could only find a non-spectating stage. As we walked past this big sign which said 'No Spectators', we bid a 'Good Morning' to all the Irish Guarda. One of the guards had just put up another sign with his hammer and nails when he dropped his whole bag of tacks all over the road! With that, whistles started blowing telling us the first car was coming and there were tacks everywhere! It did cause a panic!

These police were a real hoot. It was summer time so they wore sandals instead of shoes... well, it was hot weather in June!

Another year later, Ian retired. The service crew went and found them and the rally car and Ian went over and asked one of the guards, "Where are four thirsty fellas going to find a drink at this time of day?"

The Guard said, "Oh, I don't know, but I know where five will!".

Ian Oldfield

84 – Donegal Yarns – Our first visit to Donegal

Our first attempt at tackling the Donegal Rally was pretty successful. It was great going with Yuk as they all knew him over there and the locals were really pleased to see him again.

Me and Lou Naylor won Class One in my little 999 Mini Cooper. At the prize giving, we were the first people called up to the stage to get our prizes, of course, and the locals treated us like heroes and literally carried us over their shoulders to the stage! They made you feel great and so welcome. It was a big deal for us – our first international rally, 320 stage miles, 200 and more competitors and a real adventure. It was 1977 and we were very young.

When Yuk got his trophy, again they carried him high over their shoulders to the stage with such a loud cheer you would have thought he had won! They loved him over there and as far as they were concerned, he was a legend!!

We realised actually it is a mistake to complete all three days as you miss out on so much fun during the day in the bars! All the spectators and crews who had retired all had a great time!

On a night time, there was such a lot of fun going on. Someone found a hosepipe in the garden of The Ballyraine Hotel where we stayed at and decided to put it through any bedroom window which was open and soaked everyone and everything! You just got no sleep!

At the entrance to the hotel was an 'in and 'out' system – only someone in a little Fiat did not quite make the gap in the entrance and had smashed into one of the posts, so it was left there all week! No-one bothered; they just used the 'out' instead! No-one seemed to think about shifting it out of the way!

Overseas in the BMW

One of the many Mini's

Yuk's first RAC Rally with Eddie Ganderton

1991 with Crofty

Rarely in a straight line on the Mintex

Mind the rock!

Yorkshire's Yuk Hodgson is on the brink of retiring from rallying. Simon Cooke tries to find out why.

Every sport needs its characters. Football has Gazza, snooker Hurricane Higgins, and tennis John McEnroe. Rallying is in grave danger of loosing one of its most colourful characters, Yorkshire's larger than life Yuk Hodgson.

Yuk, a regular competitor in the Gold Star and Clubmans championships and a member of Yorkshire's rallying mafia, has his faithful Escort up for sale and looks destined to retire at the end of the year, another victim of the recession.

"It's a vicious circle," he explains in his broad Yorkshire accent. "I need other people to be buying parts from me so that I can afford to go rallying myself, and there just aren't enough customers around at the moment."

For the past 25 years Yukspeed's main business has been buying, breaking and selling rally cars, specialising in Escorts, but business has shown a steep decline in the past year or so as the recession bites.

"It costs me about £1000 to take part in an event, but you have to draw the line somewhere and decide enough is enough, and I'm at that stage now." Hence the 'for sale' notice on his much-loved Escort.

Always good for a quote, *Rally Sport* decided to take a chance and ask him what he thinks is wrong with rallying in

ENDANGER

Colourful character

Donegal again – an old favourite

Tony Coward

85 – Donegal Yarns – Last minute!

Ireland was always unique; everything was always last minute. The start ramp is just one example. They wanted to put car number one on the ramp ready for the morning, so at about 5.00pm the day before, they lined up this Porsche 911 to go up, but the angle was too great! Everybody was supposed to be going over this the next morning of course, so the organizers got a team together to build another two smaller ramps to go at the front and back of the main ramp and spent all night building these things up!

We were stopping at the rally HQ in Letterkenny and the hotel was having a big ballroom extension built onto it. The rally prize presentation was going to be in this room, when they got it finished!

Yuk had stopped there the year before and had promised to bring back 30 visitors for the rally, which he did. The hotel manager was good friends with Yuk and welcomed us in and boasted of this fantastic extension he was having built. He was so proud of it and couldn't contain his enthusiasm as to how brilliant it was going to be and, as he walked us through to this building site, they were laying concrete!

There was no plaster on the walls, no wiring, not even a proper floor! We couldn't believe it. He said, "and over there will be the bar, and over there the stage... " This was a week before the presentations would be happening.

The night before the prize presentation, we sneaked in to have a look and sure enough the floor was down, the walls were plastered and painted, the bar was there, everything was up...they had done it! Mind you, it was a challenge going to the loos! Chris went to the loo and found that the cubicles were up but there were no doors and the toilets themselves were just sat on the floors... but not fastened down! It was ok; they were at least over the holes!

When we left, the hotel owner gave Yuk a case of poteen to say thank you! This drink was so strong Chris and I could hardly drink it. We had a get together at Bill Lumb's house after the rally back in Yorkshire and they had a roaring open fire, so I chucked Chris's drink on the fire and woof !!! as it went up the chimney it was like I had thrown petrol on the fire! I thought I had blown the roof off!

This particular year, Yuk had his old Cortina estate as a service barge which he also used for the pace note checking too. We all went along together in this car to have a look at the stages. In this old Cortina he had a Country and Western tape and when you started the tape the first song began with the sound of a telephone ringing. It would go "bring, bring....bring, bring....bring, bring....and then a voice would say "hello?" Then, there was a pause before the song started all about telephones.

Yuk had brought along an old black telephone hand set and fastened the telephone line under the dashboard somewhere. Now bear in mind this was 1976, car phones and mobiles did not exist then for the general public, but police cars had radio phones, of course. On the recce, we approached this road junction and there was a telephone engineer working on one of those green boxes on the island by the junction, so Yuk pulls up to the junction and with the windows down started the tape, "Bring, bring...bring, bring." This engineer turns round and Yuk answers the phone then passes it to this guys and says, "it's for you," and the engineer takes the phone off him and says, "hello, hello?" The timing couldn't have been better and sure enough the tape then says, "hello"... So the engineer is shouting down the phone, "hello, hello, is that yourself?" We were in hysterics!

The service areas in Donegal could sometimes be absolute chaos! One we went to was down a small track, maybe one and a half car widths, which was reasonably workable if all the service barges parked on one side of the road. What made it more difficult was this lane received cars from both directions as they went off to do stages firstly in the north up the lane and then came back again to go down the lane, this time to do the stage in the south, each time receiving service.

Where we were servicing there was a bungalow which had an 'in and out'"drive, so I said to Mucky Bob, "Shall we go and have a word with the owners and see if we can use a bit of their driveway?" The old couple that lived there were sitting in the window watching all this chaos going on. I went and saw the couple and they were fine with this so we put the barge a little way up the drive and Yuk could then pull up the driveway a little way and be completely off the road.

Most service barges did park on one side of the lane, but inevitably (this is Ireland, don't forget) some didn't! This caused so many problems as it created all sorts of bottlenecks. Anyway, two constables turned up, so I had a word with them and said, "If that van moves to the other side of the road it will really free up a lot of the problems here."

They replied, "Oh, we can't do that sir!"

"Why not?" I said.

"Well, that's the local mayor's son and he can park anywhere he likes."

I couldn't believe this so I asked him if I could go and ask him to move.

"Oh yes, we don't mind if you ask but we can't..."!

Then the constable came up with a plan: "Tell you what, we will make you Special Constables for the event, then you have plenty of power!"

They got their notebooks out and took our names: "Tony Coward and Rob Nowell, Special Constables for one day!!!"

Sure enough, we went and talked to each of the service crews, and no problem, they moved their vans and a lot of the problems were alleviated. What did the two coppers do? Went and joined the old couple in the bungalow and watched from the window too with cups of tea in their hands!

Later on, they came out of the bungalow for a chat. I asked the police sergeant about tyre laws in Ireland at that time, regarding tread depth on ordinary road cars because I had seen some cars on the road where the tyres were down to the canvas, even the police car had bald tyres on! The sergeant looked at the other constable and said, "Go on, tell the lad," and the constable says, "To be sure, if there is any tread anywhere at all on the tyre its legal, even if it's painted on."

There were road cars running around in Donegal with no wings on, just the inner wing and strut going up and down. Nobody bothered!

Lovely people, lovely part of the world and completely unique.

86 – Co-driving for Piggy again!!!!!

Piggy couldn't find anyone to do the Manx in his Gp.A Mitsubishi Starion so I ended up with him again. The car was ideal for tarmac and had originally been built for the circuits but was then converted to rally spec.

We booked in to this flash hotel (Piggy always did it in style as you now know!). I met up with one of the top co-drivers (think it was Mike Broad... I think!) and he says, when making notes don't do more than five lines on a page, so you don't get lost as you bounce around in the car... good tip that.

It turned out at Rally HQ there had been a load of amendments to the stage routes which I didn't know about. So we go out to recce the route in Piggy's big Jeep and we are going round the Island and at this road end, we keep seeing the same crews over and over coming out from our left. Piggy says "Why do they keep doing that?"

I says, "I don't know; keep going."

Anyway, we get back to the hotel and we get talking to these Irish lads and mention this. They explain, "Yuk, you've been taking the wrong route, buddy; they've changed it ages ago!"

One day, we get back in to the hotel and we get a note which was left in our pigeon hole where the keys were, saying, "Practice car so and so, please go and see the Clerk of the Course." We didn't know what this was all about. It turned out one of the marshals going home for his tea tried to follow us and we had been clocked doing 100 mph in this little Jeep!

Piggy says, "There is no way we were doing 100mph. It's only a little Jeep!" Thing was – it had been all tuned up with a turbo and chipped up, all sorts!!!

So we get out onto the stages… well, I shit myself! How anyone sits next to me at those speeds with their head down… I take my hat off to them. So we do the first stage… it has this long, long straight, with loads of gravel on the sides of the road, telegraph poles and trees and things… I shout out, "hairpin right at the end." Well, he just ignores me and I'm thinking fucking hell, when we get to the end we are going to have an enormous accident! Somehow, we get round and finish the stage. The marshals take the time and I have no idea what the time is; I'd forgotten to stop my watch!

So, we start the next stage… 50 yards up the road and 'bang', the car stops. Thank fuck for that, we can retire!

We walk back to the start and there is an ambulance parked up. So we sit in the back talking to a nurse and she says, "You're shaking!" She was dead right; we had just done a hundred million miles an hour down a stage – of course I was shaking!

87 – Rallying with aristocracy!

The Honourable Henry Howard was one of the famous Howard family from Castle Howard, near York. The big house has been famous for years for being filmed for the TV series, 'Brideshead Revisited'. Henry was the nearest thing to royalty that Piggy and I had come to meet. He was always good value and proper posh, I mean *properly posh!* Very 'old money'.

Piggy and I met him for the first time when we went shooting on his father's estate. Henry didn't have a gun himself as they had banned him for having one when he nearly shot the head game keeper by mistake, thinking he was a pheasant behind a wall! "I gave him two barrels," said Henry!

He came to the Manx Rally in 1988 for the first time. Piggy was in his ex-circuit racing Mitsubishi Starion Turbo again and this time had Craig Thorley co-driving. I was spannering with Tiddles (Pete Fidell) and Henry joined us. He had only ever seen one rally before, the old Raylor Rally ten years earlier, which started outside the family home and had a stage down his driveway and round the estate.

We once again stayed at this very smart hotel on the Isle of Man which Piggy had booked and we were all togged up for dinner in the evening. Henry was sat with us and the waiter came round taking our orders. I ordered a steak, Piggy and Craig said what they want and then Henry said he would have the duck.

"What type of duck would Sir like?" says the waiter.

"Any type of duck, just duck; do I have to come and cook it myself?!!"

I suppose that is how he was brought up to talk to staff.

Piggy is sat at the dinner table in his smart, double-breasted suit and Henry says, "David, just undo your bottom button when sat at the table." Etiquette – you see! He was always putting us right, but he was really interesting to talk to!

So, we get to the end of the meal and it's time for the port. The glasses came and were set out in front of us. Well, this wasn't right at all for our Henry.

"I'm afraid we need to change these. You have given us whisky glasses, not port glasses."

We are left waiting ages but finally the staff come back again and lay out some different glasses and pour out the port.

"Well we will have to put up with these sherry glasses; we can't be waiting any longer!" says Henry.

The next day, me and Tiddles set up service at the Grandstand area whilst Piggy and Craig went off to make their notes. Piggy had new brake pads fitted but they needed bedding in, so I said I would take the car down the road... and Henry could come for the ride. So what do you do? Go down the road at 100 mph, stamp on the brakes, warm 'em up, cool 'em down, warm 'em up, cool 'em down and so on. Henry has got his posh flat cap on, his pipe in his mouth and a box of Swan Vestas trying to light his fuckin' pipe! He kept missing his pipe every time I stamped on the brakes!

"Yukky! Will you stop doing that! He's the only person to have ever called me Yukky!

I said, "Look Henry, I've got do that."

There was tobacco and matches flying all over the place! So I stopped and let him out and I tell him I'll pick him up on the way back. Well, I drove back to the service area forgetting all about him. "Where's Henry?" says Tiddles.

"Oh fuck I've left him behind!!!"

Later that day, Henry's getting restless stood in the service area and says, "It's five to twelve – time for a drink."

He wobbles off to the hotel on his own, leaving me and Tiddles to get on. Henry looks great wearing one of my Yukspeed T-shirts, his flat cap and his pipe.

Finally, me and Tiddles get finished and go and find him in the bar talking to all the Motoring News reporters and photographers with a load of drink round him. Tony North (the well- known rally photographer) takes me to one side and says, "Who is this guy?"

"Why?" says I.

"Well we've bought him all these drinks and he hasn't bought one back! He says he's Piggy's Team Manager!"

At the end of the rally, Piggy and Craig had won an award and it was time for the crew to go up on stage, but Craig had disappeared somewhere, so I says to Henry, "Go on Henry, go up with Piggy and pick up the award." Henry stumbles up there after having a few, takes the microphone off John Horton who is compering and does this fabulous speech. You would think he had won the rally! He had everyone laughing and cheering; it was fabulous! Still, no one knew who the fuck he was!!

On the ferry coming back from the rally, there were some technical bods from Honda motor cycle racing team who had been there the previous week for the bike racing. They were doing a survey on what people thought of Japanese motor cycles, Honda in particular.

We were all spread out on seats not feeling very well after the previous night's drinking and they went up to Henry and said, "Do you mind telling us what you think of our motor cycles?"

Henry says, "I hate the bloody things!" So the Japanese gentleman writes down, "I hate the bloody things".

"And why do you hate the bikes?"

"Because they frighten my pheasants, now fuck off!"

Sadly, Henry died about 9 years ago, but I often think about him with real fondness and a smile on my face.

Motoring News reported as follows on the rally in the 27th March 1988 edition:

"David 'Piggy' Thompson and Craig Thorley took third in class in David's Mitsubishi Starion, although the turbo pipe came off early on and they had no turbo boost. It was a useful result and one made all the more remarkable bearing in mind the considerable handicap of having Yuk Hodgson co-ordinating service arrangements! Ably assisting were the infamous 'Rubber Doris with the infamous suspender belt' and a certain member of the aristocracy who answered to the name of Henry!"

So, how did you get the name Yuk?

I was christened Yuk!

---

88 – James Thompson rally rookie

In the early 2000s Jimmy (Piggy's son) decided he wanted to try his hand at rallying. He had enjoyed loads of success in touring cars but fancied a new challenge and he had always wanted to go rallying. With some support from Peugeot, he had the use of a proper Gp. A 206. Naturally, I was around to help out and service the car.

He had to do a few small events to get his experience on stages like anyone else, get his correct licence signatures and so on, so he entered a local single venue event on Melbourne Airfield. There was quite a crowd stood around this works car in the service area and one bright spark says in a loud voice, "Oh, it's that touring car tosser that's driving this!"

But Jimmy was stood just behind him and turns round and says, "Oh, that'll be me, then!" Cool as a cucumber just like his Dad was!

In 2002 he had a Gp. A Mitsubishi on loan from Ralliart. We did quite a few events that year and we had a good little team looking after him. I used to take a nice bit of Christmas cake with me to hand out to the lads – keep them motivated, like! Well, this Christmas cake I have had for years; it was lovely – all sliced up with a bit of cheese; must have been at least 10 years old!! Think I have some left now! They all loved it!

Piggy was not so well by now so couldn't always make it to all the events, but I made most of them when I could to keep an eye on young Tommo.

89 – Piggy's 24-hour wake 2003

Taken from the Yorkshire Evening Press Feb 27th 2003:

'Piggy' inspires 24-hour wake.

Tributes have been paid to David 'Piggy' Thompson, who died earlier this month, aged 57, after a long battle with cancer.

The respected businessman, rally driver and former pig farmer – where the nickname came from – was remembered by more than 400 family friends and colleagues at his funeral service, held at St Mary's Priory Church, Old Malton, last Thursday.

David was well known in the York area for his pig farm at Earswick – at its peak the largest of its kind in Yorkshire.

Married to Barbara, 62, the couple spent more than 35 happy years together at Fosslands Farm.

He was also a talented rally driver, winning three British titles in the 1970s and 1980s. He will be best remembered for his performances in his Porsche, and last competed competitively in the RAC Rally in 1995, aged 50.

David was also proud father to professional racing driver James, 28, who last year won the British Touring Car Championship, and is this year competing in the British Rally Championship.

When James' career began to take off in the mid 1990s, David realised a long-held ambition by moving from farming into engineering, as well as property development, building more than 100 homes in the village.

His engineering firm, Foss-Tech, began life in one of his former pig barns and grew to a 22-man workforce. The firm designed and built the Honda and Audi touring cars, which James raced in Britain and Germany, and is now a successful firm producing precision parts for the racing car and aviation industries.

David was also a prominent member of the National Farmers' Union, a keen country sportsman, and a big supporter of the Malton and Norton Rugby Club, often enjoying tours abroad with the team.

Friends have described him as a "unique man, with so much drive and determination, he could achieve whatever he set out to.

After the funeral, David's friends did their best to carry out David's wish of a 24-hour wake, celebrating his life in style at the Malton and Norton Rugby Club before heading off to some of the favourite pubs, finally ending the night at 4am.

90 – Fuck it, he's lost me bucket!

Jim Kitson was a red hot co-driver when we did Donegal but a fuckin' rubbish spanner man in France! We were doing the Charlemagne Rally.

We had come into service and had a check over and I says to Jim, "Get a bucket out of the van and give the race car a quick wash down."

"We haven't got a bucket!" says Jim,

"Yeah, we have – it's in the back of the van!"

"No, we've lost it!"

Jim had flung the bucket over the wall into the river and the fuckin' knot had come undone on the rope and the bucket went floating off down the river never to be seen again! It was probably blocking the fuckin' shipping lanes about an hour later!!

91 – There have been accidents!

TR7 V8

I can't remember ever crashing Escorts, but that TR7 V8 gave us a frightener! We had done the Mintex in February and, amazingly, it was bone dry! We did right well, 14 o/a with Alf. It had a hell of a pace on the Dalby straights... well, well over the ton mark on those straights going for 6th gear and had a wobble on over a crest!

A month later was the York National and we came up to the same crest and there was a crossroads with gate posts; I was slightly over to the left. The fuckin' thing took off and we spun 360 degrees in the air and landed... Luckily, it landed at this fork in the road and we ended up in the bushes. So I backed out and carried on, but a few yards down the road the oil light came on; we had damaged the oil cooler!

So we parked up and I walked back to the junction. "Was that you in that TR8?" said some spectators.

"We have never seen anything like it! Your car took off and spun 360 degrees in the air and did it twice!"

Fuckin' 'ell, I thought. I must have blacked out after the first one!

I was going to sell the car after the rally to a fat lad from Thirsk way. He came up to watch the rally. He was called Kevin Kettlewell. We had agreed on £6000 for the car so I got the car repaired and ready to go, when he rang up saying his Dad had seen a cheaper one down south – nearly two grand cheaper! They went and bought that car instead. I don't know how many engine rebuilds they had but they saved themselves two thousand quid! I bet they spent more than that getting the thing sorted! Every time I see poor old Kev I say, "Well, if only you had bought the right car!"

We also rolled the car on the Gems Brock at the stage finish on an airfield with Half a Brain (Mick Dent) co-driving. We had about 200 yards to stop, and fuckin' hell, it didn't! I chucked it sideways, touched a fence and she rolled over into this field on the roof. I clambered out, but then Half a Brain's wallet comes flying out! I thought, I'll have that!

When I got the car home, I found out the problem; the brake balance had vibrated to the back so there was no braking at the front. No wonder we went flying off! Luckily, there wasn't too much damage though!

Manta 400

We had a small accident down in Wales in the Manta 400 with Amos (Andy Moss) co-driving this time. It was one of the first rallies I did with the car. It was early on in the event and we had been to service and went to the next stage and there was this long, long, long uphill and over a crest...We came over the crest then 150 to 200 yards before a square right, with logs on the outside. We never had notes then so we were still working from maps. Anyway, under braking I says to Amos, "You had

Manta damage not too bad!

better hang on – we aren't going to get pulled up for this!" I chucked it sideways and we slapped hard on into this big heap of logs which were end on to me. We went bouncing off the logs and we are seeing bits of plastic flying everywhere off those lightweight wings the Manta had!

We got going again but the front wing started to rise up in front of us; we couldn't see a thing!!! I decided to stop and have a look. It had taken the front wing off, the back wheel arch off, but never touched the axle, so we carried on to the end of the stage.

Andy says to me, "Well, I have done some rallies Yuk, but I have never done one where I am told to hang on so early in the event!"

Rally Sport magazine December 1987; report Premier Cambrian Rally (European Motorsport BTRDA Championship)

> "Car 28....Yuk still has some way to go before he feels fully at home with the Manta but was still good value for money as he brought his battered Manta home 14th overall after several brushes with the scenery."

I mentioned this accident to Piggy when I got back. I says, "I can't understand why I crashed, Piggy."

He says, "I'll tell you why you crashed; it has more power and you were going faster over the crest than you are used to, taking it flat in an Escort would have been fine but in the Manta..."

That car was so much faster than I was used to, everything happened so much faster. It was pushing out somewhere around 270/280 bhp and loads of torque. It had a 2.4 engine and it put the power down better. It was a really nice car that.

BMW M3

My worst accident though has to be in the M3 on the Tour of Flanders with Baz Dove. When I got it, Piggy said to me it would take 1000 stage miles to get used to it!

It was a last minute deal to go to Belgium and we went across with Chris Barker and a mate of his who did the spanners for us. We had to do a loop of three stages then come back into service. There was nowt to do with the car and Baz was reading off the pace notes perfectly. He was cool and calm and mint.

We came out of service and I was buzzing now. We headed back to do the same three stages again, so I says to Baz, "Tighten up your seat belts, we are off to start motoring now, Baz!" He thought I had been going a bit steady for him, but I was just starting to warm up!

So, we are coming down this straight and we had 200 or 300 yards before a square left next to this bungalow. I hit the brakes quite late. It was a narrow road with a couple of feet either side, and a bit cambered. It pulled me onto the grass on my side and into a ditch! There was this brickwork there holding a drainage pipe. My front wheel was pulled right off and it bent all the inner wheel arch – folded right over so there was a six inch gap between the transmission tunnel and the inner wing, and pushed into the brake and accelerator pedals! Luckily, my feet were pushed outwards rather than inwards, otherwise I would have lost them if they had got trapped!

The car barrel-rolled onto the road and landed on its wheels! Baz was still reading his notes! I couldn't get my door open, my seat had come up and my knees were tight up against steering wheel. So I climbs out through my window and Baz had to do the same. But I couldn't stand up because my ankles had gone funny.

I was lying there in the grass and the car behind me was blowing his fuckin' horn... there I was lying on the grass bloody dying!! The grass had just been cut and then burnt down so I was lying on these ashes in my white OMP suit...I thought, "Why, old devil's got me already!!!"

The ambulance came and they put me on a trolley and carted me off to hospital where they did a series of X-rays. They says to me, "Stand up."

I says, "I can't, I'll faint!"

Anyway, they insist I do, so I stood up and keeled over and fainted! Bloody told 'em!!

So finally they brought the X-rays back and said, "Which is right and which is left?" I hadn't got a clue! So they said, "Well, there is a fracture there! Oh well, we'll pot up both them!"

I can't believe they didn't know which foot was left and which was right!!

When we got back to the UK with the bent race car on the trailer, I hid it away for a week or two because didn't want to look at it!

The BMW not so good!

It took nearly a year to get fully recovered. It was hard trying to get around let alone run my business. But looking back I was very lucky. I still get problems with my ankle to this day, especially in winter.

I re-shelled the car in the end. Bilko rang me up. He had heard of a touring car shell in Nottingham, all caged up and ready to go. It took some copying – all the little special bits and pieces from the old car onto the new one, but it was good as new when we got her finished.

92 – Navigators/co-drivers

I have had loads of co-drivers over the years. I think the main reason why I have had so many is I have never had a major sponsor as such. I have looked to my co-drivers to pay the entry fees or what they could anyway and most can't keep that expense up every month, so I have had a few because of this!

Jem Hodgson (my daughter)

Sue Lamb (Jem's mother)

Adrian Wilson

Alan Andrews

Alan Edwards

Alf Smith

Alison Stansfield

Andrew Henrey

Andy Moss

Ann Watson

Barnacle Bill

Baz Dove

Bill Lumb

Bilko

Brian Parkin

Bryan Pickles

Chris Walker

Christine Coward

Christine Parling

Colin Essex

Dave Curry

Dave Elcock

David Curran

Dr. Nick.......... no, can't remember!

Dermot.................can't remember his surname; Andy Elliott's mate!

Eddie Ganderton

George Barker

Harry Bodge

Ian Jemison

Ian Oldfield

Jim Kitson

John Birkett

Joe Cruttins

Jonathan Pulleyn

Julia Rabbett

JS Hargreaves

Kate Richardson

Kevin Bardon

Kevin Carruthers

Lou Naylor

Mark Wareham

Mick Dent

Nigel Cay

Peter Croft

Paul Howarth (Yep, the Prodrive man, Paul Howarth!)

Paul Skinner

Pete Slights

Pete Stansfield

Phil Shaw

Pip Dale

Rick Francis

Richard Nightingale

Richard Stark

Rob Pilcher (*Just one stage; shouldn't have, but he jumped in the car at the start of a stage without telling us!!!*)

Roger Butler

Stephen McNulty

Steve Shaw

Terry Wilson

Tony Coatsworth

......and loads more I have probably forgotten about!

I always like to take any new navigators out for a run in the car before an event to get them used to the noise and speed of the car. I have had a few over the years who've been a bit shocked early on and maybe not been at their best straight out onto the first stage. A quick run up the road beforehand helps them get used to it.

I do like my co-drivers to be organised to give me the confidence to get on with the driving. The last thing I want to do is try and sort them out as well!

93– Memorable co-drivers

Craig Thorley

We were doing a forest event – Hamsterley, I think it was. The rally was on maps. Well, Craig has his head down reading the road all the time; he never ever seemed to look up! Anyway, I have this enormous moment and we go off into a ditch on the inside, bouncing along having quite a big moment and he barely flinches. Finally, I get the car back onto the road and sorted it out like and I shouts, "Will you fuckin' look up for once and admire my driving!"

Dudley Dave

Me and Dudley Dave did Donegal in the Rothmans-liveried Mk. 2 Millington. We went over to recce the stages and check out our notes. As we were going along, he kept saying to me, "high tea." After asking him to repeat it about three times, I had to stop and I say, "Dave, what are you saying 'high tea' for – we have just had a big breakfast?....high tea what?"

"80…..80 yards to the next corner," says Dudley Dave!

Well, he was a Brummy!

Once we got started on the rally proper, poor old Dave struggled to keep up with me. I finished one stage before he had!

I always say to navigators to write things down for the service crew to check out at service. That way we don't forget and we can get things sorted before we go out again. On Day 2 the gear knob came loose. I got it fixed at first service, but a few stages later it comes loose again. I said, "Just jot it down so we can tell the lads again to get it fixed." We are just about to leave service again and one of service lads asked after the knob; it still wasn't fixed!

By this time, I thought I would have a quiet word, so I takes him round back of service barge and says, "Look Dave, I've been quite patient with you, now there is a reason why I want you to write things down."

His answer was, "It's hard to write things down at 70 mph!"

I says, "It's fuckin' hard to change gear with no knob at 100 mph!"

We get to the last day and we are doing ok; we are 2nd in class behind Jeff McNeil in his Mk. 2 Escort BDA and an Irish Cossy is 3rd about 12 seconds behind us. I says to Dudley to keep checking the times of the Cossy so we know how we are doing.

First stage, we took 5 seconds out of him, second stage he got 2 seconds back on us, third stage we get 2 back, fourth stage he gets 3 back on us. For the final stage, we all have time for a natter. The Cossy driver says to me in his Irish twang, "It's close now, Yuk. We are only 2 seconds behind you, my friend!"

I says to Dudley, "Go and check the times with your Cossy navigator, 'cos something is wrong there!"

He comes back and confirms we have only got 2 seconds on him.

"What's happened to the 12 seconds you say we had on him?!!!"

"Oh, I was checking times with the wrong co-driver who is in a Vauxhall!"

Now it's time to give him a right Yorkshire bollocking! "How can you be so fuckin' stupid with only one fuckin' head!"

I never drive quicker than I feel I need to, so now I have to stretch my ability on the last stage. Half way through the stage, I see a car in the distance (maybe 15 seconds in front, as we were running at 30 seconds intervals)... I think he must have had a problem at a bridge where we had a moment too. We keep pressing on and catch him just before the finish line but did not get delayed... and we just did it! Second in class... phew! I didn't enjoy those last few miles at all; I am not into driving faster than my eyes can see!

Paul Howarth

Me and Paul (Prodrive) Howarth did the Silva Stages in 1993 in the BMW. There was always strong competition between a few of us up there in Gisburn Forest and I loved doing that event. Me and John Morton were always pushing each other.

I couldn't believe it when, on the very first stage that year, as you started the stage, the road went sharp left then a long uphill right hander that was like the edge of a three pence bit. Poor old Mort had gone off on the long right! As we came past, his car was stuck in this hole at a real awkward angle and 'Mort was propped up against car legs 'akimbo' trying to get her out! By, it did look funny; I couldn't stop laughing!

"Will you stop laughing and concentrate on the road!" shouts Paul, but I just couldn't stop giggling all way to the end of the stage!

Anyway, old John got his own back on us 'cos we retired later with a bust exhaust when we were lying about 5th overall.

Peter Croft

There are not many navigators I've had I could rely one hundred per cent on (in the car) but Crofty (Peter Croft) was one. He was a super man for organising me and the confidence he gave me once I got to know him was second to none. That left me to get on with the driving and not have to worry about other things. The first rally we did together was Northallerton Motor Club's Christmas Stages Rally in December 1990. We retired after three stages because it was just sheet ice and snow.

We achieved loads of satisfying top ten finishes in 1991 and 1992.

In 1993 I bought the M3 and our first rally was the Seizoen Rally in Belgium. We got 9th overall and also 13th overall on the Charlemagne in France. On the Seizoens we were on one stage when Crofty gave me a great mouth full of notes coming onto a 800 yard straight! Going onto a reasonably long straight gave me chance to have listen to the car which means I didn't take a word in! "Repeat..." I says,

"Told you once, I am not telling you again!" was his reply. He did then duly repeat, but when we got to the finish I was still pissing myself laughing!

I says, "What was all that in there then?"

"I'd turned my page over" was his reply!

That was the year I started wearing the amber tint driving glasses. We arrived at the start of one of the special stages and the marshal tells me that I am not allowed them with an open face helmet, so had to hide them until the next stage.

At the end of '93 I crashed the M3 and was out of rallying for eight months. In the meantime Crofty had found a ride in a 4x4 Sapphire.

One chap commented Crofty was mint in the car and crap in the bar! We went to our local pub and sure enough Crofty was first out of the car, but as soon as we got to pub door he stopped and bent down. "What are you doing Crofty?"

"Tying my shoelace!" was his reply!

"Crofty you don't have any, you've got slip-on shoes!" I told him he'd need to get up earlier than that to catch me out!

Top man. RIP Crofty.

So, how did you get the name Yuk?

There was three of us from Gate Helmsley: Chuck, Nuck and Yuk; 'Chuck' who was Charles Richardson, Noel was called 'Nuck' and I was called 'Yuk'!

Craig Thorley
94 – That was a late call!

I have only ever done two rallies with Yuk but spent hundreds of hours in his and Piggy's company.

The first time co-driving for Yuk was in one of his G3 Escorts on the Tour of Hamsterley. The rally was on maps and I was still doing lots of road rallies then and was pretty handy on the maps. As I sat in the car, this giant Brantz trip meter was right in front of me so I turned it off. We set off on the first road section and I had my head in the maps when Yuk pipes up, "Hey! Why is the Brantz turned off? That cost me a fuckin' fortune... get it turned on! I want to see it flashing and beeping!"

Once onto the stages, we were flat out down a long straight. As usual, I had my head down reading the map. I was repeating the words, "Straight for one mile... straight for ¾ mile"... when the car started to bounce half into the undergrowth and half on the road! Bushes were hitting my side of the screen, but I kept my head down and repeated, "It's still straight!"

Yuk looked across at me and said, "Get your head out of that potty thing and admire my driving skill!"

I looked up for a moment and just replied, "It's a straight!"

Well that's my version!

Our second event together was the fabulous Plains Rally in Wales.

Another side of Yuk came out on this event – his love of animals. When on the Sweet Lamb stage, we drove past a lamb which a previous competitor ahead of us must have clipped. When we got to the stop line, Yuk was distraught. He told the finish line marshals they needed to stop the stage quickly and get somebody in to see to the poor little lamb.

Once again, we were still on maps but this time we were in the BMW M3. The car had been rebuilt following Yuk's big accident on Flanders. His confidence had taken a knock, understandably, and he wasn't driving like we all know Yuk could drive.

As the event progressed, I decided to try to push him on a bit. He still wasn't reacting like I knew he could, so at a square right I waited 'till the last moment and shouted, "Square right"!

"That was a late call youth!" said Yuk, after we had scrambled round the right hander!

"No, that's where we are supposed to be braking!" I explained!

Ian and Christine Oldfield
95 – By, he's a cheeky one!

Ian: *Both Christine and I got to know Yuk when he was a window cleaner in Stamford Bridge where we both lived even before we married. He used to come to my mother's to clean the windows -always at a lunch time, so then he could have his lunch which she made him!*

Christine: *Then he would go to either my mother's or my Auntie Freda's, clean their windows then say, "Is there owt in pantry missus?" The number of times they would say, "By, he is a cheeky one that Yuk Hodgson!" but he always got away with it!*

Ian: *Christine and I had just got married when I bought a Mini rolling shell off Yuk which he had been using himself. Lou Naylor built me an 1100 engine for it and Lou and I did a few events together. I've got to say the car was a 'shed'! It kept blowing fuses! I found out why. Yuk had put a nail in one of the fuses instead of a proper fuse! I couldn't understand why the battery kept melting!*

The car had a little light on the roof and a policeman pulled me up once and wanted to know what this light was for. "No idea!" I said. When you're young, you don't really give it a great deal of thought!

Christine: *It used to slow people down if we were following them because they thought we were a police car! The car had this little light on the roof and the car was painted light blue with a white roof which was a typical police car colour in those days!*

Ian: *I rallied another Mini after that one and usually bought any Mini bits we needed from Yuk. Then we all moved on to Escorts and I did the same then too, of course. He ended up* buying my last Mk. 2 Escort (SBT) which by then had a 2.2 BDX in it. It had been through a few hands including Peter Hodgson (not related to Yuk – from Doncaster!) and James Holmes too. I think Yuk broke the car but kept the engine because it was a fabulous unit.

I navigated for Yuk on quite a few rallies over the years. In 1980, we did the Lindisfarne Rally and did really well. We finished 8th overall, just beating Piggy with Mike Wood in his ex-works Escort (GJN 126T). It was a Castrol Autosport/ RAC National round with some serious opposition but Yuk never put a foot wrong all day. Every stage he was not the fastest but always put up really good times and clean driving with no mistakes. Kielder always seemed to suit him.

We did Otterburn as well, the Crystal Stages and loads more events. I don't know how I ended up doing so many with him! He must have been desperate, got me pissed at the motor club so my resistance was low, and then persuaded me to sit in when he couldn't find anyone else!

He hated it if you moved at all in the car! You would be going down a straight and he would bray you on the leg, shouting, "What the hell's that for?" And he would say at the finish, "Oh, on the second corner you moved your leg!"

"Oh, did I?" He was often dead grumpy with you.

You would be flying down a stage and the concentration would be full on and no-one saying anything. Then, he would say out of nowhere,

"I crashed there last year!"

He would love a laugh off the stages, but on them he was always deadly serious and focussed! He was a quick driver especially when he was in his forties and he could still see! He was always consistent and rarely crashed.

He has never invested in decent tyres though, which make his results even more impressive! Often the tyres didn't even match! If he'd had decent tyres, I bet his results would have been even better!

We had some great times in the bar with Yuk over the years. There was always something happening! The year Prince Charles and Princess Diana got married, the whole country had a day off and we started our celebrations with a bit of a session in the pub in Fangfoss (a little village outside York) and carried on that night in the York Motor Club clubhouse at Dunnington. We had that much to drink and we were that knackered that when Ginge (Nigel Cay) chucked some drink over us we just couldn't be bothered to retaliate. Yuk *always swore he would get him back one day! Of course it took years and years to do it, but he finally did get him back with the washer pipe incident in to Nigel's helmet! Classic Yuk!*

Me and Yuk always met up in the bar on a Wednesday at the motor club, sometimes on a Thursday and sometimes on a Tuesday as well! Friday and Saturday night – always! And then Sundays at the Three Cups in Stamford Bridge at lunchtime! By we did sup some stuff!

On a Wednesday night after the club bar closed at 10.30pm, we would rush into York to a lovely, ancient pub called The Black Swan on Peasholme Green. When that shut, we would head off to Andy Elliott's hotel for more drink and then on to his night club, Ziggy's, for even more!

One night we came out of The Black Swan and there was this single decker bus coming along the road which had 'no service' on it and was obviously heading back to the bus station for the night. So Yuk flags this bus down, opens the door and says to the driver, "where are you going?"

He says, "I am off back to the depot."

Yuk said, "Oh, you couldn't just drop us off, could yer?" and this lad takes us to Elliott's Hotel in completely the wrong direction for him, nowhere near the depot!

So, Yuk asks this guy to take this big red bus down to Sycamore Terrace where Andy's hotel was (a very narrow street in York with residents' cars parked at both sides). "I can't take my bus down there!" says the driver.

"Course you can, you'll be right!" says Yuk!

Yuk and I get out and the poor guy took about fifteen minutes to turn this big bus round! He must have thought what the hell am I doing here?!!

Every night I was out with him something ridiculous happened! If it was his turn to drive, we never took a direct route home. He'd say, "Oh, it's a beautiful evening, let's have a ride round!" We never went straight home!

He would ring me on a Tuesday late afternoon for example and say "Are we off out tonight?"

"Yeah fine, but I am still at work, so let's meet at half seven."

"Oh no, that is far too late! I'll pick you up at six and we will get home early!" he'd say.

The only early we ever did was early hours of the morning!

I will never forget what he and Piggy used to do to poor old Diesel Jack! Diesel used to get right annoyed at them because they would sabotage his wellies by finely cutting around the wellie by the ankle but not at the front, so when he came to pull them on they would snap off! He went looney and wouldn't speak to them for months!

We could drink in those days and boy did we laugh! There was always something happening! Yuk Hodgson, what a legend!

Huddersfield Chris (Chris Walker)
96 – What have I just said?

My first event co-driving for Yuk was the Leeds Crest Forest Stages, in a red Mini Marcos (a plastic thing).

I went across from Huddersfield the night before the rally to help with the final prep of the car. Putting a roll cage in a Tupperware vehicle doesn't kind of fill you with confidence!

We were at Bill Lumb's place, Escrick Service Station, where Yuk was based at the time. Leaving the garage at 1.00am, we were stopped by a police car just 200 yards up the road heading towards York. Yuk greeted the officer by the words, "What the fuck do you want, you silly old git?"

Now, I thought that wasn't a good way to talk to an officer of the law when you have a bed of your own. If, on the other hand, you are homeless, it may just pay off! The policeman replied, "Oh it's you Yuk, just wondered who was coming out of the garage at this time of night!"

Thankfully he knew him!

Next morning, the rally took us up into the lovely Yorkshire forests in what was a fairly quick Mini Marcos. The first 'Jesus' moment we had, we got it crossed up at high speed in the fast straights of the Harwood Dale stage. When we got to the finish line Yuk said, "Bloody hell, I was a bit worried there!"

I secretly thought, "Well, if he was worried at that point, at least we have similar worrying bits, so this might be a good ride!" It was.

Later on in Wykeham Forest, we went down a rabbit hole on a banking but luckily recovered and went on to win our class by the end. The event finished at the Crest Hotel in

Oulton near Leeds. I don't remember the night do but I do remember the headache next day!

Our second event was the Gwynned National rally in Wales in a Mini.

A wheel, a Mamba four spoke thingy, shattered – possibly on a rock or something on the inside of a bend in a very icy Penmachno at night. There was still quite a way to go so we pulled in and I went into the rear of the car to release the spare. The next thing I knew, a bunch of Welsh guys came out of bushes and rolled the car onto its side in order to swap the wheel... a much quicker way than jacking! The gentlest roll I ever had. I don't think we won 'owt on that one!

On the 1979 Mintex International, Yuk was co-driven by Lou Naylor. I was co-driving for the late Peter Ripley, a quick Huddersfield driver who campaigned mainly Toyotas.

It was a real snowy rally. The whole route had to be ploughed that year as it had snowed really badly in places and many of the stages were almost or totally impassable. As a co-driver, it was the hardest thing I had ever done with route alterations being posted almost throughout the whole night before the start. It was a co-driver's nightmare! Mike Nicholson, who was co driving for Pentti Airikkala, and who was later to become head of Vauxhall Motor Sport, was stood next to me at the amendments board and said, "They should just cancel the bloody thing"... and that was from a top professional!

After scrutineering, I went home in the Toyota rally car with Peter via Leeds and bought all the OS Maps covering the route before returning to Harrogate from where the rally started. I went in my own car so I could keep an eye on the route alterations. I had nowhere to stay, but Yuk came to the rescue and I finished up in his room with about eighteen others – some of whom were men!

Peter and I won our class with Yuk and Lou second. I thought this would be my finest hour. To be awarded the class win on an international rally and going up onto the huge stage at this big posh Harrogate hotel at the awards ceremony – with the likes of Hannu Mikkola and Pentti Airikkala looking on! However, when the announcement came for the winners, the computer print-out had omitted Peter and I from the results! The award was presented to Yuk and Lou!

Yuk went up and told the compere over the microphone that he had not won, but took the award after being shown the results sheet by the official on the stage. When Yuk got back through the crowd to where we were, Mr Ripley looked like he might have a go at Yuk, but before you could crack a whip, three or four burley York guys politely explained that it may not be a very bright idea to do so!

I did get my trophy about two weeks later after the organizers, De Lacy Motor Club, had sorted their bloody computer out, but I missed the moment. The trophy, by the way is the only one I have on show at home and it still has Yuk's finger prints on it!

Huddersfield Chris loves Yuk's perm!

The next event I did with Yuk was the Summer Stages Rally run by Robin Hood Motor Club at Fulbeck Airfield near Newark, using Yuk's yellow Mk. 2 Escort BDA.

This turned out to be the first event Yuk ever won outright, beating David Bell and Steve Johnson also in Escorts – and they were the lads to beat at the time. John Wilcox Racing Engines supplied many of the top lads in that area and they were very competitive. Yuk had a Tony Drummond built motor in the car and there was quite a battle with Steve Johnson who was supported by Wilcox, so it was a straight fight between a Wilcox engine and a Drummond engine. The Drummond engine won and we were pedalling it!

Coming back up the A1, Yuk must have been thinking about the win when he suddenly burst out, "Fuckin' hell, no beer last night, that's how you must win!"

I don't know if that is the trick, but it worked on that occasion!

Our fourth event together was the Donegal International rally in 1982 in the TR7 V8, the ex-works British Leyland beast. The Terratrip was wrong and I had to guess at what mileage the stage notes took effect. Yuk said, "You're not happy with the 'trip', are you?"

"No, we are going to kill each other mate!" I said.

"Oh bugger it," he said, "you look round the right hand bends and I'll look round the left hand bends!"

That was typical of his attitude.

We came a cropper, however, on stage 9, after very long airborne jump and an almost vertical landing which broke the track control arm and anti-roll bar. God knows how we didn't go end over end! We repaired the car that day and entered the consolation race the day after on the Sunday and promptly won! We even beat Vincent Bonner, who won the main event the year after in 1983. We had an excellent few days, nearly drowning on Guinness. That car, incidentally, did four mpg! I still have the service info in the tulip book somewhere. Nearly as bloody thirsty as we were!

A previous Donegal, in 1977 I think, I was part of the service crew with Rod Wood from Huddersfield and Lou Naylor from York. Bilko (Mike Jackson) was doing the driving and 'Jimmy's Legs' came with us! 'Jimmy's Legs' were the two prosthetic legs Yuk had taken in part ex for a train set or something! These were strapped to the roof rack with the spares on the service barge. We had 'Jimmy's Legs' poking out from under the rally car handing them spanners, much to the dismay of the Irish spectators who were puzzled to say the least! We must have been a bit daft as the legs had no arms!

Yuk was in a Mini with Bill Lumb as co-driver. The car broke down and had to retire, so we set off to retrieve Yuk, Bill and the car. Although we found the car, Yuk and Bill were nowhere to be seen (no mobile phones then) but bugger me, they were in a farm house slurping a tot or two of whiskey! We then decided to start the evening's slurping for real in a small village pub and asked the landlord if we could bring 'Jimmy' in. The legs were placed on a buffet and we bought 'Jimmy' a half... the landlord seemed puzzled too!

It was in that bar that Bilko (who many years earlier as a young lad had sadly lost his right arm in a car accident) fell soundly asleep! Mike detested cigarettes so that prompted us to let him have a fag! We lit this fag and stuck it in his false hand without him knowing! I'm sure somebody took a photo but I don't know who!

That was the year Ari Vatanen was co-driven by Peter Bryant and after another very long night necking Smethwick's beer, someone decided to put the hotel out with the fire hose, even though it wasn't on fire! The result of which was a very damp hotel!

In the early hours, there was a knock on our door followed by a voice,

"This is Mr McGarvey, the manager."

... so Bill Lumb filled the waste paper bin with water to let Mr McGarvey have it... but as the door was quickly pulled open, there was Peter Bryant... a Ford works co-driver for probably the best driver in the world at that time! Anyway, he got the full bucket! However, he did manage to smartly throw in the fire hose which was on full blast trapping it in our room with the door closed on it!

Needless to say, that night it was like sleeping in a lake! The real Mr. McGrarvey gave us on our departure back to the UK, a few bottles which we opened on the ferry. We had passed through the army posts in Belfast with guns pointing at us through the turrets of the checkpoints. Another rally to try to remember!

One year on the Scarborough Stages, I was in a hotel with my crew as I was doing the driving on that occasion in a Cortina GT, when a dishevelled, duffle-coated urchin peered through the room window. It was Yuk! Within half an hour or so, he was lolloped in a chair and we were pouring beer down a hacked off rubber plant leaf into his head. God knows how we drove next day!

I think it was the York National rally (maybe early 80s) that Yuk and I ended up having ten over the eight. It was the night before an early start and we were in very good spirits! God knows what time it was – I guess about one-ish in the morning and competing in that rally was works Talbot team manager Andrew Cowan.

Yuk and I found a wheelchair from somewhere and started racing down the corridor of this hotel where the bedrooms were either side just like a line of trees down a fast straight in Dalby! Yuk was pushing and I was, of course, co-driving in the seat. Anyway, we rolled it!!!! Yuk went flying arse over tit and I could even see what shoe size he took as he flew past me in the air!

We were laughing our bollocks off when a very annoyed and very Scottish Andrew Cowan appeared. As his bedroom door flew open, he was in a pair of 1918 baggy underpants and a string vest! His hair looked as if he'd just got out of bed or something; he certainly hadn't combed it – to absolutely bollock us! But when he saw the wheelchair and Yuk – face down in an ashtray and me with my foot stuck in one of those new-fangled automatic shoe polisher, Mr Cowan calmed down a bit and then shouted, "Come on lads, it's fuckin' loads o'clock in the morning!" We eventually went to bed and eagerly awaited the headache to come!

Yuk is undoubtedly the most talented driver I have had the pleasure of co-driving for. He was also the craziest by a country mile, but when the countdown reached 'Go', he was a different Yuk, very nearly sensible! What have I just said?

Lou Naylor

97 – Come on Louie – don't be fuckin' about!

I got to know Yuk at Stamford Bridge where we all lived, when I was only eight or nine years old. This would be in the sixties. He was friends with my brother. They were all in to Minis, as was everyone in those days and Yuk was massively into them. A whole bunch of mates would meet up at my parents' house because we had a big garage which we used as a workshop and I can clearly remember Yuk having his engine in bits and fitting a new crank with the help of all his buddies. I was fascinated and learnt such a lot; maybe that is why I run my own garage for a living today.

Sandocross racing!

We would all go off to the big autocross events which ran in those days, such as the Players No. 6 events at High Eggborough, where Yuk was racing against the likes of legends such as 'Jumping Jeff' Williamson, and Yuk did really well against these guys. He bought a green Mini Cooper S with a white roof, twin tanks, inch and half SUs, all the right gear and used it at a Sandocross race meeting on Filey beach racing against people like Mad Dan Grewer. It was great to watch, just like an autocross but on a beach – sand flying in all directions and would you believe it, Yuk got FTD (fastest time of the day)! We were all chuffed to bits! The car was not the most reliable though and the front suspension collapsed on the way home!

When he was running his business from Escrick Service Station, he rang me one day to say he had a problem with a customer's Mini. He told me he had rebuilt the engine and fitted it back in, but when he came to firing it up, it wouldn't start on the battery, only if he push- started it. I said I would come down that night and take a look. Everything seemed fine on quick inspection and sure enough, once we had push-started it, the car seemed fine but just would not fire up on the starter. Eventually, I realised why it wouldn't start when you cranked her up. He had fitted an old starter motor he had on a shelf in his workshop, which turned out to be for a Dolomite not a Mini and it was turning the engine the wrong way round!

I co-drove on a few events for Yuk. One of the biggest events has to be the old Mintex International rallies. The first one was in his Mini Clubman. He drove that car with such vigour! We did Oliver's Mount in the snow one year; well, he hardly had the car in a straight line around the whole stage! Great fun!

We did the Mintex again together in 1981, in his yellow Mk. 2 BDA and we were in the top twenty and going very well with lots of top names competing like Vatanen and Mikkola in Sutton Escorts. We arrived at the Otterburn Ranges in the dark for service. Like everyone else that night, we assumed the stages would be dry as the service area was completely dry and we put racing tyres on. But when we headed up onto the tops, the roads were covered in snow and ice! We came to this valley and it was almost a traffic jam – cars off or stuck all over the place trying to get back up the other side! Yuk says, "Get out and give them a push!"

So I was out there, pushing other competitors up the hill when Yuk saw a gap and decided to have a go at getting himself up the hill. He found grip on the grass at the side of the road and passed lots of cars who were waiting to get up, as I am coming hell for leather down the hill on this ice in my trainers! I was trying to stop but couldn't! I slid straight into the front of the car, bang into the bonnet, over the bonnet, hit the windscreen and came down onto the road at his side! He shouted out of his window, "Come on Louie, don't be fuckin' about!" and he carries on up the track leaving me behind! Once he had got the momentum he was not going to stop!

When I set up in business, we both had workshops next door to each other at Gobbo City in Elvington. One late afternoon Yuk saw me and said, "Do you fancy a pint tonight, Lou?"

"Yeah, I do," I replied.

"Let's go around town. You come round to my house and I'll get cleaned up then we can call at your house and you can get cleaned up".

I had a jar at home which I used to save fifty pence pieces in and loose change. Anyway, we set off into town after I had got changed and the first pub we stopped at Yuk says, "I'll get these." So we have our first drink of the night, then we go on to the next pub.

Yuk said, "I'll get these; you put your money away," and he buys the next one. So there is me thinking what a swell guy he is! He keeps buying all the rounds, all night. Next morning I see him at work and he says, "Did you enjoy last night buddy?"

"Yeah," I replied. "I had a great night – really enjoyed those beers."

"Well," he said, "you bought them, out of your jar money!" The cheeky bastard!

For all Yuk's wild and cuckoo style of life, there is a really soft side of Yuk which came out on the Mintex which started from Harrogate. We were all waiting to go when he spotted a lady across the road in her Mini estate. She was clearly heavily disabled and was struggling to get out of her car. He ran over to her and asked if she needed a hand. She was delighted to be asked and in a shot, he had the wheelchair out and was carefully lifting her out of the car and into her wheelchair. It was lovely to see and I was touched by that.

Billy Ballcock (Dave Elcock)
98 – Billy Ballcock – the sausage jockey!

My very first rally was with Yuk. It was a bit of a steep learning curve! It was the Stockshill Scarborough Stages in Yuk's 3 litre Capri in 1979. The rally started from Scarborough, of course. We got the car scrutineered, then straight off to the bar and got pissed as usual, which was basically the law when with Yuk!

We were staying at the rally headquarters, The Prince of Wales Hotel, where everyone was staying. We had a grand night but next morning once we got in the car and up to the start ramp, Yuk says to me, "Which way, Billy?"

"I don't know Yuk," I said. " I'm still pissed and got a hell of a hangover. Just head for the first stage which is Oliver's Mount!"

Yuk says, "Billy, we have got to follow a proper route!"

I says, "Find your own way there Yuk, no one will say anything, they all know you!"

Yuk says, "Look, I don't know how to get there either, I'm still pissed as well!"

Anyway, somehow we found our way to the start of the stage at the bottom of Oliver's Mount. Quite how we managed it, I just don't know! When we arrived, we saw two young ladies that we know, called 'Map 100' and 'Map 101'! We nick-named them Map 100 and Map 101 because one came from Malton and one came from Pickering! In fact those maps never covered that area, but it always sounded better!!!

So we are queuing up for the start of the stage when a commentator sticks his microphone through the open window under Yuk's nose, "Now then Yuk, how are you? I see you have a new navigator, who is it?" Now this is being broadcast to a very large number of spectators all gathered around the motorbike circuit;

"Awww," says Yuk. "This is Billy Ballcock, he's the local sausage jockey!"

... and I'm thinking, bloody hell I don't really want to be introduced as that around here!

We hurtled around Oliver's Mount or Oliver's Clit, as Yuk would call it, but every time we came up to a bend which came up fast and we were hard on the brakes he would hit my leg! "Stop moving your fuckin' leg!" he would say,

"I'm not!" I'd shout.

"You are, keep your fuckin' feet still!" Once we finished the stage, he told me to stop moving my feet around. I told him I wasn't!

"I know what it is," he said. "It's your trouser legs flapping about." No overalls in those days!

After the Oliver's Mount stage we headed off out of Scarborough towards the forests and after the Dalby stage, we went through a small village called Snainton, which at the time had a little bicycle shop there. So Yuk pulls up, switches off the engine and says, "You stop there." And off he went in to the shop. He came out with a pair of bike clips! For the rest of the day I had to wear these bloody bicycle clips! What did I look like?!

He has always hated navigators moving around at all. We did another local event (The York National maybe) a few months or so later which included Oliver's Mount. In preparation for the event, I said, "Look Yuk, when we get to Oliver's, you know your way around there. Can I just sit back and wave to the spectators?"

"No, you bloody well can't, keep still!" he said.

So I thought, sod this! I got a stick, some rags and a glove, stuffed the rags into the glove and stuck it on the end of the stick. Yuk knew nothing about this until we got to Oliver's Mount and as we were driving round, it was like the royal wave on the side window where he couldn't see it! Yuk still has it in his workshop to this day!

Yuk and I did some pretty big events in the eighties. I reckon we did about thirty rallies in total together. On the National and International events around that time there were lots of trade sponsors around such as spark plugs people, the brake pads people, various oil suppliers and so on. They were all willing to give you free of charge various goodies and wares for displaying their company name on the car. It was always my job at scrutineering to go and find what was available and scrounge whatever I could. But I often found these suppliers saying to me that Yuk had already been around.

I am certain he knew what he was doing, making sure he got the freebies and then selling them on later!

Scrutineering was always a nervous time. You had to make sure you spoke to the scrutineer nicely because there was always something dodgy about the car! There was never a mechanical handbrake for example, which you were supposed to have, but he would bluff himself through it somehow!

Service could be a stressful time for me because he would always be off buying or selling something and could I never find him when we needed to be off!

We did The Lindisfarne Rally in 1981 which used 'Killer Kielder'. It was my very first visit there and there were no legal pace notes in those days, just maps. The problem with these maps was that the accuracy at times left a lot to be desired. If you competed often there you would know the bad places, but I didn't have a clue where those places were.

Yuk was flying this particular day. We went round a square right, we were flat out down this straight and I could see these three brows coming up towards us at a fair old rate! I glanced down at the map at the first brow and shouted, "flat!" and it was... come to the second brow, "flat Yuk!" No problem... come to the third one, "Flat Yuk." But over the brow was a little pond and the road went left around it!

"Awwww, shit!"

Well, you can always tell when Yuk is in trouble because he starts whistling! All I could say was, "Stick to the road... Jim!"

Anyway, he stuck to it alright and we scrabbled round the corner just and we both pissed ourselves laughing! We laughed so much as we went down the next straight, the car was all over the road. We fell off on the next corner!

Yuk and Billy Ballcock wait to leave service in Scarborough

We did the Mintex together in the Gp. 4 Escort NWR 184V in 1983. One of the stories from that event was me and Yuk getting a really quick time on Croft only a few seconds down on the great Stig Blomqvist in his Gp. B Audi Quattro. The truth was Stig did the stage in thick fog; when we attempted the stage it was almost clear! Still made a great story in the papers!

Sue Lamb

99 – In the dog basket

I met Yuk at Lavarack's Industrial Estate or Gobbo City as Yuk liked to call it. The company I worked for had an industrial unit there and I sometimes took my car to his garage for repairs and got talking to him. Lou Naylor's unit was next door to Yuk's and there was loads more little units all next door to each other, all great lads. I was the only girl based there working in the office on the estate. They all used to like to have a bit of banter. Even though I would be only about twenty years old, I could hold my own with these guys.

I bumped into him at one of the night clubs by chance and ended up taking him back to my flat opposite the Bar Walls in York. He dashed across the road and got me a handful of daffodils which were growing up the banking planted by York City Council. He was quite romantic in some respects, even if they weren't his!! He would take me for a surprise lunch sometimes on the spur of the moment. Sometimes we had sponge and custard, which was our favourite.

I kicked him into touch when I found out he had another girlfriend and never told me, so we had a big fall out. Anyway, he came round and we ended up going back out and eventually we ended up living together.

Wednesday nights he would go off to the motor club and then into town. One night I turned up and he was not happy because it was his night. "What are you doing here?" he said.

"So? I thought I would come and see you," I replied.

"Well, its Wednesday night, it's motor club night!" I got told off!

We had been together a couple of years when he asked me to do a single stage venue rally with him. I wasn't keen on doing the bigger events, but I did occasionally do more major events like the Sligo Stages Rally. We had a few wins such as the Christmas Stages. He loved me being involved and supporting him. He especially wanted to win if we were competing, so he could say, "Me and Sus won that." He wanted to do the same with Jem as well. He was keen that she could be proud of what they did as father and daughter. Competing as a family meant a great deal to him. It was like a reward for all the things we did together.

He is an extremely safe driver. I found it fascinating to sit and watch him. I couldn't bear the thought of reading pace notes to him, but on single venues I just had to direct him. His co-ordination was amazing and I felt so safe with him.

He could be quite demanding at times. Things had to be right. I know Jem found that hard at times when with him, so I always went along too to make sure she was on the ball and knew what was going on. But she is very capable with pace notes, far more so than I was.

I remember him buying a 900cc motorbike when we were living at Spitalbeck. I thought God, I don't want to go on that, but sure enough when I did get on I felt safe. He once bought me a trials bike for my birthday! It was great fun, but I could never kick start it on my own!

I was always good at organisation so I would get the entries in, book hotels, organise food and so on. I loved the rallying; it was always great socially. It got me away from work and was such good fun. We would leave for Wales or Scotland or somewhere miles away. We would have a party pre-rally and then the next night a post-rally party! It was always fun and usually with the same load of friends we all knew and it was all very relaxing; Ian and Christine Oldfield, Derek "Booler" Parling and Christine Parling and so on. Then we would pack up and head home on a Sunday; we had great times. Everyone knew Yuk. People from the rallying community would come and say "hi" after meeting on rallies or coming to his workshop to buy parts.

Once we had set up at Barton Hill, Yuk's working day could be very long because customers would call on a night for parts and he would work all evening sometimes and over the weekend too.

If customers turned up late on a Sunday morning, at lunch time we would close up and say to them, "Right we are off to the pub, are you coming?" The customers were usually friends anyway! We would have a session in the bar, Sunday lunch or a BBQ and carry on drinking for the whole day! We both knew how to party!

Our local pub, the Spitalbeck Inn, knew when we were in as Yuk usually got up to something! One night he put a banger into the brass tube that ran around the bar! He could screw the end off and pop a lit banger into it then pop the end back on….BOOM!

I organised a surprise 40th Birthday party for him at Barton Hill, but I had to do all sorts to make sure he was there. He decided to do a rally that day but his engine was not ready, so I tried to persuade the engine builder not to have the motor ready, but Yuk insisted that it would be ready! I was desperate to make sure he came back on time as I had about seventy to eighty people invited! All those people managed to keep it secret! So, then I had to ring the organisers to let them know what I was up to, as the event was only over the Pennines from us.

I came up with this story that the workshop had supposedly got broken in to and that he had to come back straight away as the police had caught them but could only keep them for so many hours and we needed him to identify the stolen goods. Anyway, the *plot worked and he came home to be greeted by this massive party! He was so taken in he took some persuading that nothing had actually happened! We had such a party that night!*

One memory I have of living together is that he had been rallying and got home really late. I had gone to bed, but got up when he came in and I made him a hot drink and a sandwich. He then decided he needed something stronger to drink and got himself a whisky. I locked up and said, "Right, I am going to bed."

"I'll be up in a minute," he promised.

I woke up a bit later on and wondered where he had got to. I went downstairs and there he was in his rally overalls still and his head lying in the dog basket! The dog looked up at me and was trying to say, "For goodness sake, will you get him up to bed!" He loves his dogs!

Although I was a lot younger than him, I was never really aware of it; he never grew up! We had some wild times with a huge number of friends – a lot my age or younger, in some cases. I had to grow up when Jem was born; that did not come easy for Yuk, though! By the time Jem was three or four years old we decided we needed to split up, but that never stopped him being a good father to her. Because of his lifestyle, he could go and pick her up from school when I was working and she would stay with him regularly too and still does. He has been the most incredible father ever.

We are still the best of friends. It is almost like a brother and sister relationship now, always there for each other if needed. He loves his dogs but he loves his family and friends too!

100 – Rallying with Jem

After my first visit to Jersey I fancied having another go at it but in my own car this time! I thought it would be good fun for me and Jem to do it in my Mk. 1. Trouble is, it is such a very, very expensive event to do. Flying out to the Channel Islands is not cheap. In 2008, I said we would do it.

The problem was you have to go over the week before to make your notes, and then you have to go back home and the following week you have to get your outfit over there. Anyway, Jem's Mum, Sue says she will pay for the hotels for us and we start to make our plans. Then we found we couldn't get an entry! It filled up so fast; it's a popular event. Anyway, I flew over just for the crack, but it was a shame really that we never got a go at it.

Proud Dad

I was chuffed to bits when Jem showed an interest in competing. I built this Mk. I Escort and Honda engines seemed to be the way to go for affordable power. A few lads in Ireland were trying them and I could see a market for conversions of Escorts to Honda power. After all, my Vauxhall conversion kits had worked really well in the past and still do.

A local lad, Spinky (Richard Spink), was after building a Mk. 2 and going the same route, so we worked together on developing the kit.

I painted my car red and gold like the old Alan Mann Racing colours. It turned out I wasn't the only person who liked those colours as Peter Smith (Swift Caravans) who had been retired from rallying longer than me was making a return in the same colours, except his car was Mk. I Pinto in historic spec! There he was – twenty four years since he had last rallied and suddenly he appears in this lovely looking Mk. I – put mine to shame! It was immaculate!

Jemspeed was brilliant from the moment she started co-driving. She had no apprenticeship, she went straight into a full house Gp. 4 Escort, no experience of notes, no training; she is a star!

Me and Jem did a few events in that car. On the Jack Frost Stages at Croft we had a bit of a misfire and I struggled with a poor dog box. I did the Riponian with someone else and it was so slippery we had loads of spins; it was unusual to be going forwards! For the Humberside Rally, I had Jem back with me and the event gave us a retirement with a broken box. I have never been so happy for a box to break – I hated the thing! After the Chatsworth Rally Show event, me and Jem did the Dukeries Rally in the June. It was a red hot day. We had done a stage and there was a smell of oil under the bonnet. I stopped and found out it was the breather on the gearbox. I must have over-filled the box and it was dripping onto the exhaust. We backed off a bit and got the car to service where we could drain a bit out.

We then goes back to do the same stage again, and I remember it 'cos it started on tarmac with some wooden huts at the side of the road. We set off into the stage and everything was going good when all of a sudden the road just disappeared. Now what was on the notes, I don't know, but we just never lifted... took it flat... and we were in mid-air for weeks! Luckily, the road was straight... I says to Jem, "Hang on!" We could have had a right good chat before we landed! Fuckin' hell, it landed perfectly!

Later that year, we did Hamsterley and exactly the same thing happened again!... big dip... "Hang on Jem!" I have never seen any photographs of the Dukeries or Hamsterley of those incidents but someone, somewhere must have some! The best I got was one off Steve Pugh and we were only about an inch off the ground in it! Pughie says,"I am never good with yumps!"

We have done some spectacular things over the years! On the Malton Forest Stages a couple of years back in the Millington Mk. 2, we had pulled 18 or 19 seconds back on the second man in class (Andy and Dave Gibson I think it was). After 3 stages in the afternoon, we were really on it and it was the last stage of the day, we went into an open chicane, square right, square left and I know Jem said, "Don't cut."

I just chucked the car in expecting it to slide. It went round the square right alright but on the left, it didn't. The car just dug in and went up on two wheels! When it landed, it bent the steering arm, but I didn't know; the steering was trying to pull the car into the ditch. Woah! Slow down! What a shame, as we were only 1 second behind the Gibsons by then.

About four months later I was talking to a customer, "By Gum Yuk, you were lucky on Malton Stages!"

"Why?" I says.

"I was on that chicane junction and you went up in the air; all I could see was the underneath of your car!"

"Did you get a picture?" I says.

"No I was too aghast. I have never seen owt like it!"

I asked him what happened 'cos I was never sure why we just went up so quickly onto two wheels. He says the ruts from the four wheel drive cars had made us dig in and to nearly topple over, but yet again, no picture!

I tell you what though, Jem never flinched!

Jem Hodgson
101 – Playing Gypsies

Having a Dad like Yuk is pretty mental! There is never a dull moment! He always has a good story to tell or some daft idea we should try. When I was little, we used to play in the back garden and my Dad would build a fire in an old alloy wheel, we would make tea and toast on it and pretend to be gypsies.

From a very young age, I would sit on his knee on the lawn mower whilst he cut the grass. I remember crashing the lawn mower into the plum tree when I was five and Diesel Jack ran over to rescue me. Dad couldn't wait to get me into driving cars and bought a grass-tracking Mini when I was ten. I never competed in the car but had loads of fun playing in it around the garden and up and down the local farm tracks. Of course, it wasn't long before he was teaching me to do 'J' turns and handbrake turns!

When he decided to return to competition, I couldn't believe it when he asked me to co-drive for him. I had been used to being around his rally cars and trophies all my life, but the thought of actually competing with Dad was so exciting. He had two new seats made up for the Mk.1 Escort he was building and when they arrived and we unwrapped them, I saw on one seat he'd had embroided "Yuk" and "Jem" on the other; it made my little heart go!

Our first event together was the Malton Forest Rally in 2007. When we got to the long Dalby Forest stage and came hurtling down to the famous wood yard there must have been thousands of spectators cheering us on, it was so exhilarating knowing they were all there for us! Dad has so many followers and friends who would ask, "What is it like competing with this legend?" He makes me very proud.

My favourite stage we ever did was around Oliver's Mount on the Kall Kwik, which was part of the Roger Albert Clark rally in 2008. It is one of my Dad's favourite stages and as we were coming up to the start I said, "Dad, I am not too sure how to read this stage to you." He simply replied, "You just sit back and enjoy it, Jem."

JP (Jonathan Pulleyn)
102 – Christmas at Croft

Yuk had not rallied for quite a while. He had been suffering badly from sciatica.

Yuks Facebook timeline Nov 2013 read something like this:

"Went to watch Malton rally last w/e, mint to get talking to lots of folks on stages which were fast and dry. Bumped into Larry Carter who informed me that the Northallerton Motor Club's Christmas Stages was filling up fast (have put entry in). Thanks to JP for driving me. His reward is to sit in with me at Croft!!"

Andy Forrest:

> *"Look forward to seeing you and JP on the Xmas Stages – when is your book out?"*

Miles Cartwright:

> *"Knew it wouldn't be long before JP got back in a rally car after the Stivie Stages!"*

Andy Forrest:

> *"Just hope JP does not bring his sundial stopwatch!"*

Pete Stansfield (Bottles):

> *"Reward?!!"*

Steve Wilson (Animal):

> *"More like punishment!!!"*

Yuk:

> *"Shhh, Bottles, or I'll tell 'em about the time your crash helmet fell over your eyes on the yump at Oliver's Mount!!"*

Pete Stansfield (Bottles):

> *"That was your erratic driving!"*

Christmas Stages 2013 – Croft Circuit, by JP

It was Larry Carter's fault! He got talking to Yuk on the Malton Forest Stages Rally when Yuk and I were out watching. He told Yuk how entries were filling fast on the Christmas Stages Rally and how it was going to be one of the best yet; that got Yuk thinking... never a good thing! An entry was put in quickly. Then I got an email from Yuk saying as a reward for taking him to watch the Malton Rally, I could sit in the silly seat with him on the Christmas Stages! Some people said, "Reward?!!! Don't think so!"

I couldn't wait for Christmas. I love the Christmas holidays anyway but it's even better when you have a rally to look forward to. As some of my friends might remember, it was over thirty years ago when I last co-drove as opposed to driving, then in 2013 I had the pleasure of co-driving Peter Smith's beautiful Chris Birkbeck prepared Opel Kadett on Malton Motor Club's Stivie Stages in the summer. That was an epic day, and one I shall never forget. Now I had chance to enjoy it all over again with Yuk in his usual light blue full Gp.4 Mk. 2 Escort powered by a Millington Diamond motor. Mint!

The rally was on the Saturday between Christmas and New Year so on the Friday, Josh (my youngest son who started co-driving in 2013) and I went over to Yukspeed at Barton Hill to help load the van. Josh was down to service along with Billy Split Pin (Kevin Bardon) from Kirkbymoorside.

The van was loaded up with spares and the rally car popped on to the trailer ready for a ridiculously early start on Saturday! "See you at 5.30am-ish outside your house JP," said Yuk. How early?! We had to be at Croft for scrutineering at 6.45am as we were seeded at 35.

Saturday

It was a slow and quiet journey in the van to Croft on Saturday morning! Too early, man!

Anyway, Billy and Josh got things laid out next to the van and Yuk and I trundled down in the rally car to 'Noise'. No problems there and then we joined the queue for the scrutineering hut. It still felt very early, so much so Yuk and I both nodded off a couple of times whilst waiting in the dark and quiet!

Safely through scrutineering and now signed on, we had an hour and a half to prepare ourselves. The stages looked very similar to last year's when Josh did it with Pete Williams (there are only so many versions I guess on a race circuit!). I had a wander down the service area and caught up with a few friends. I saw the Mellors boys and a few others including Peter Smith who had put a late entry in with his new and very smart red and white tarmac spec Metro 6R4 run by Pete Slights and said 'hi' to Ash and Emma Slights, who were servicing.

Christmas Stages 2013 with JP

I met Alan Oldfield (brother of Ian and Dave Oldfield) for the first time too. He was pitched up next to us with his smart Darrian.

Finally, it was time to get strapped in and get in the queue for the first stage. Bugger – she wouldn't fire up! The battery was flat. "Right lads get pushing!" shouts Yuk and within a few yards she had fired up fine. Once up to the start line, I see an electronic clock to count us down and I thought we never had that in my day!

"Count me down Jon," says Yuk.

"Ummmm, not sure how this clock works... ummm... 5, 4, 3, 2, 1, Go!"

Oh well, got that bit right and off we shot! Up to the first hairpin left which takes us on to the circuit and we are flying, hard on the brakes into the first right in front of the grandstand, into a square left and hairpin right... the car weaving, under braking then slightly sideways out of the bends under power... a lovely feeling! I was pressed down hard in to my Motodrive seat. I had forgotten how nice it was to compete once again. This was mint!!

We blasted up the circuit, weaving between the natural chicane, then up to the next chicane which took us left off the circuit and round the back of some buildings, then back on to the circuit again... down to Tower, a long tight right hander, then chicanes again before coming to the first split. "Keep right, Yuk," I shouted.

"Don't shout Jon," he said. I had forgotten that these Peltors work so well!

We came round to another chicane. This one was particularly tight and Yuk gets it slightly wrong and we have to reverse; bollocks!

Then it is round the back of the circuit, hairpin left around the back of the pits and garage buildings. Yuk gets this spot on, a quick pull of the handbrake, power... beautiful! This was such fun! Yuk can still really, really drive a Group 4 Escort despite his lack of practice recently!

After two stages it was time for the route to be changed for stages 3 and 4.

"Now I've woken up, JP," says Yuk. "I never go well in the morning or in the dark."

"You mean you can go quicker?" I thought!

Our battery issue was sorted when one of Yuk's customers/mates, Steve Popey, came up and kindly supplied him with a brand new one in exchange for a few stickers on the car. Thank you Dynamic Battery Services.

Third Stage

The third stage was something else! Yuk certainly had woken up and was really driving with some commitment now. He was quick before, but now – well this was really showing me what he can do! I was still trying to find my feet after so little match practice myself, to suddenly finding Yuk absolutely on it. We finished SS3 slightly breathless (both of us) but also noticed the car sounded like she had just dropped onto 3 cylinders. "Mmmm, what is going on here?" says Yuk. We pull in to service and Billy and Josh raise the bonnet whilst Yuk scrambles out to investigate.

A whole bunch of people gather around, all keen to see what the issue is. Chris Mellors of MEM comes over. He knows his way round a Millington, of course.

He pulls the plug leads out and checks everything he can think of including the injectors. After a few minutes of trying a few things, Yuk fires her up and all seems well – hurray!

Off we go for SS4 and it still seems fine up to the Service Out control, after which we switch off when it becomes obvious we are going to be held in the holding area for some time. When Yuk fires her back up to pull up to the stage start, she sounds sick again. We decide to set off and see if she clears, but no… after one lap we pull in and gain a maximum. More work under the bonnet and more people pile into help including Pock from Motoscope. It looks like the injectors are at fault or possibly an 'O ring' has slipped. We are out.

My stomach feels empty and I am not sure if it is because of the disappointment or if I am hungry; it is both. I felt gutted as we were just starting to find our feet. Never mind! This has been another ambition achieved, co-driving for the legend Yuk Hodgson!

103 – Yuk's Service Barges

Another Yuk service barge

The Vauxhall Cresta's Bench seat!

When I was at Escrick in the seventies, "Fatty Jeff" who we talked about earlier in the book, used to spanner with us for Pip and Mick Dale on the RAC Rallies. He had a big Vauxhall Cresta. "E" registered, it was, so it would be a 1967 saloon model. I bought it off him taxed and tested with a tow bar on it, so this was ideal to stick the racer on the back. I had a two wheel caravan chassis converted into a trailer! Mint, it was! Cost me seventeen quid!

I used to leave the old Cresta at the side of garage when the tax and test ran out, and I could take a bird back there, start her up like (the car!) and we could get on the bench seat!!!

Bedford CF Hire Van

Pip and Mike Dale had entered the RAC Rally when it was a mammoth event and the service crew had to follow the rally all the way round. We even had to drive all the way up to Aviemore and Grantown-on-Spey in heavy snow to follow the route in this hired Bedford CF van!

Me and Fatty Jeff brought a portable cooking unit along so we could all have some hot food or a hot drink. We put it on top of this Calor Gas bottle. Thing is, it was only about a foot and a half away from the roof when we had the kettle on. Well, there were blisters forming on roof! There I was outside chucking snow on to the roof to try and cool it down! It was mad in those days driving a fully laden van in deep snow up in those mountain roads, but we did it.

The Creaking Consul Estate

I had this Consul Estate as a tow car, with a roof rack on. We could get half a dozen jerry cans and maybe 20 wheels and tyres on the roof, Snap On Tool box in the boot, plus 5 people and a race car on back!

We were driving along in this old barge and there was this creaking coming from the C pillar! Animal (Steve Wilson) was sat in the back. He says, "Ey up Yuk, there's something creaking here!"

I says, "It's probably some old mouse or something!"

"No, it's more serious!" says Animal.

So we stopped and pulled the door seal away and the C pillar was cracking! The back end of this Consul was flexing and cracking! We worked out where the back beam was mounted under the floor. It was really weak around that area.

When I got her home, I welded her up and sold the bugger on!

Ian Oldfield

104 – Where yer going? Can I come?

We were literally loading up the rally car on to the trailer (an ex-Dave Richards Autosport, Henri Toivonen Porsche 911 practice car) when Yuk calls round, "Where yer going?" says Yuk. "What yer doing?!"

I says, "We're off to Holland!"

"Well, bloody hell, can I come?"

I says, "Course you can!"

"What do I need?" says Yuk.

"You need some money and you need your passport!"

"Well, where the hell am I going to get guilders from in Barton Hill at this time?!" (No euros in those days of course!)

So, he rushed off home and within half an hour was back and off we go. He had no room booked, no tickets for the ferry, no guilders – he wasn't bothered! There was a six berth cabin on the ship so that was ok, but at the hotel he had to kip in the cupboard! He tried the bathroom first but said, "Eh, I'm not that keen on golden rain"!

Whilst we were away, Eddie Ganderton who was with us, brought out of his travel bag his favourite whisky. It was a really good one like Canadian Club. Anyway, Yuk managed to get hold of it. He took the top off it, stamped on the top and said,

"We won't be needing that anymore will we Eddie?" and threw the top away! Eddie was not too impressed because he had brought it for himself, not to share!

The rally did not go to plan for us right from the start, though. It wasn't a pace note event and poor old Catch (Andy Catchpool who was co-driving) was really struggling with the maps. We kept seeing other competitors going the other way down the dual carriageway and we couldn't work out how to get to the other side! The weather was awful and we were freezing in the rally car which had no heater. It was pouring down and we eventually went OTL (over the time limit). I was pleased to hand the car over to Yuk after that, "Will you drive it back to the hotel Yuk and I'll spend the rest of the petrol money on booze!"

Piggy and Craig Thorley in the Galant

193

With Billy Ballcock on Olivers Mount

Happy with WIA 5958

One of Yuk's Party's

The Manx 1980

The Cambrian with Crofty

Billy Ballcocks first rally with Yuk in the Capri

Ian & Christine Oldfield

Everyone's happy …

"Wardrobe" Ian Jemison

Sue on right – drunks on the left

Legend 'Bilko'
Mike Jackson asleep

Huddersfield Chris in charge

200

Fuzznag (Gavin Ruler)
105 – He's a pervert!

Yuk comes in to the pub after we finished the Crystal Stages Rally. Eventually me and my wife decided to leave and go home. Yuk follows us out of the pub and says to my wife, "Here, you don't want to go with him love, stay with me, he's a pervert!"

Mark 'Skids' Skinner
106 – The mig welder incident

I called into his workshop at Barton Hill a couple of years ago and he was working with his mig welder on an Escort shell.

"Come on Skids, let's go and get a cuppa," says Yuk and without realising it, he put the mig down with the trigger pushed down and off we go in to his house to make a cup of tea.

When we finally head back in to the workshop after having a good old natter, we find coils everywhere and it is still uncoiling itself!

"Fuckin' hell Skids, I have paid a fortune for this off Spuggy! Come on, help me get this lot back in!"

He can't have paid more than about £15 for it, but insisted we tried to get this entire coil back in! After a good try we get it snagged and had to give up! Talk about trying to put the toothpaste back in the tube! Ever the Yorkshireman!!!!

107 – The infamous sun strips!

So many people have asked me over the years what the interpretations were of the various sun strips I had across the windscreen of my early Escorts. They sometimes got me in to trouble! One scrutineer insisted I removed the letters even before we were allowed to start!

NOMUF2TUFWEDIVEAT 5

Can you work it out?

Anyway, there were two different versions:

"CLAGITSRAGULEOK"

Take the AG out of it = "CLITS RULE OK"

And

"NOMUF2TUFWEDIVEAT 5" =

"No muff too tuff, we dive at 5"!!!!

Billy Ballcock (Dave Elcock)
108 – Rally 'hangers on'

Rallying has never really had the glamour that circuit racing can provide, but we did have one young lady who was very popular with the boys. We called her "The Martini Girl" – Anytime, any place, anywhere!

She was quite fussy though, she only went with people she knew and people she didn't know!

Billy Ballcock (Dave Elcock)
109 – That gets you back!

I never had any serious offs with Yuk, but he managed to frighten me a few times!

I recently retired and bought myself an Audi R8 5.2 V10 (0- 60 in about 3.7 seconds) and thought I would take it round to show him at Barton Hill. "What have you got there Billy?" says Yuk. He jumps in the driver's seat.

So I says, "Come on let's take her for a blast."

I kept encouraging him to really floor it.

"No, I daren't, no!" says Yuk and we arrive back outside his workshop after a short run. He then suggested we take the car down to 'MG Graham's', as he calls them, his friends and neighbours who are situated at the end of Yuk's road (the now disused A64 which goes outside Yuk's house/workshop). I took over the wheel and I floored it.

"Oh fuckin' 'ell Billy, you frightened me to death!"

I says, "That gets you back for all the fuckin' times you frightened me!!!"

I have to say over the years I have known Yuk, for all the front he carries (which is a lot!), deep down he is one of the most helpful and caring people you could possibly wish to meet.

110 – I love my rallying!

I don't mind loose or tarmac, snow or fog but I hate the dark! I might have a hundred spot lights pointing this way and that way, it wouldn't make a bit of difference to me! Night time is for drinking, shaggin' and sleepin'!

I have to admit, when I build a car it's a fuckin' shed! Bits of wire and fuckin' bits here, there and everywhere! Then you are supposed to set up the geometry which costs you another £1000 pound to do. My rallying is just for fun; go away and enjoy it!

I remember me and Billy Ballcock doing the Welsh Rally in PSG in 1985. It started from Cardiff that year. We got through scrutineering fine, went for a few drinks, of course, but strangely didn't get pissed! I can't remember why! Me and Billy were sharing a room (separate beds of course!) and we were reminiscing about all our rallying adventures and stories, pranks and so on, pissing ourselves with laughter and I says to Billy, "You know what Billy... we should write a book about this!"

Billy says, "That would be a right good idea"...

Then I says, "Only thing is though Billy, the book would never sell!"

"Why not?"

"No bugger would believe it!!!"

111 – For the record

Various cars rallied by Yuk over the years

8 (*I think*) Minis
1 Mini Marcos
1 Ford Capri 3100 RS
1 Triumph TR7 V8 ex-works Per Eklund
17 (*I think*) Escorts Mk. 1, 2 and G3s
1 Chevette HS (Piggy's)
1 BMW M3 ex-Prodrive John Price car
1 Manta 400 ex-works/Jimmy Mc Rae

Favourite rally car was actually the Manta. Lovely it was – ex-McRae AC Delco car. Peter Smith of Swift Caravans owns it now. Chris Birkbeck is restoring it to its former glory! Bottom of the list has to be the TR7 V8!

International rallies or off mainland rallies entered

Cork, Eire
Donegal, Eire
Manx, Isle Of Man
RAC (*the old one!*), GB
Haspengouw, Belgium
Seizoen Rally, Belgium
Mintex International, GB
Jersey Rally, Jersey
Charlemagne, France

Events tackled with results where recorded

1974

Scarborough Stages with Alf Smith in Mini retired after SS1

Crystal Stages with Phil Welch in Mini 2nd in class

1975

Moore's Opel Scarborough Stages with Pip Dale in Mini; 1st in class

Mintex in Mini with Bill Lumb

Autumn Stages Rally with JS Hargreaves; 2nd in class

Elcar Rally with Pip Dale; 2nd o/a

Cottom Sprint; 2nd o/a. *in Piggy's green Escort Mk.1 BDA*

Tour of Lincs; 19th with David Curran

Sold one of the Minis as a rolling shell to Ian Oldfield

1976

Uniband... *in new car the ex works Mk. 1 Escort T/C,* with Lubo

Scarborough Stages

Arkle Stages

Donegal

Raylor Rally; 12th in class

Lakeland Rally with Richard Stark

RAC Rally, with Eddie Ganderton; *retired with a knackered battery!*

1977

Elcar Rally, with Richard Stark; 4th o/a

Colman Stages *in new car red Mk. 2 1700 BDA; retired*

Stockshill Scarborough Stages, with Ian Jemison; 4th o/a

Tour of Cumbria, with Christine Proctor (nee Coward); 4th o/a 1st mixed crew

Hadrian Centurion, with Christine Proctor; 9th o/a

Manx International Trophy, with Christine Proctor; 19th o/a

Sold Mk. 2 Escort to Warren Philliskirk

1979

Mintex; 22nd o/a *in Mini Clubman*

Crystal; 6th o/a *in Capri*

Stockshill Scarborough Stages; 19th o/a *in Capri,* with Billy Ballcock (Billy's first ever rally!)

Cork *in Piggy's Chevette,* with Wardrobe; retired with punctures

York National Forest Rally *in Piggy's Chevette* with Wardrobe; 21st o/a 2nd in class

1980

Gwynedd; retired..... *in yellow Mk. 2, 2 litre BDG ex Guy Lockwood/ Tony Drummond / Hepolite shell,* with Lou

Mintex; retired, with Lou

York National; 12th o/a, with Kev Carruthers

Tour of Lincs; 4th o/a

Haspengow; retired

Manx; retired

Holderness Stages; 4th o/a

Summer Stages; 1st o/a, with Huddersfield Chris *First ever win!!!!*

Ziebart Stages; 1st o/a, with Chicken! *Second ever win!!!*

Hamsterley; 4th o/a

Lindisfarne; 8th o/a, with Ian Oldfield

Norking; retired

Elcar; retired crashed! *Sold shell to John Nicholson in Newcastle*

1981

Mk. 2 yellow Escort 2 *New car built from a shell bought from Dave Oldfield.*

Robin Hood; 1st o/a, with Sue

Mintex; retired with flu with Lou!

Gwynedd; 38th was 9th until Opus ignition issues

Opposite Lock Stages; (now with Atlas/ZF box) 1st o/a

Haspengow; 24th o/a

Sligo; 24th o/a was 10th until puncture

Lindisfarne, 13th o/a head gasket and exhaust prob. with Half a Brain

Lampton Park; 12th o/a

Elcar; 9th o/a *sold car to Steve Shaw with a wooden foot, a farmer in Thirsk*

Rawlings Fruit Juice; *in ex-works TR7 V8* 19th o/a, with Half a Brain

Gems Brock; retired rolled! with Half a Brain

Northallerton Stages; retired deep snow

1982

Mintex; 14th o/a 4th in class *in TR7 V8,* with Alf (Alan Smith)

Dukeries; 18th o/a misting up difficulties, with Alf

Gwynedd; 28th o/a

Rodger's Carpets; retired crashed when lying 13th o/a with Phil Shaw

Whickham; 7th o/a

Donegal; 1st o/a Sunday Run, with Huddersfield Chris

Reckitts Stages; 2nd o/a

Sold TR7 V8

Bought Mk. 2 Escort ex-Fred Brown car NWR 184V

Holderness Stages; 1st o/a

Lindisfarne Stages; 5th o/a

Lampton Park; 3rd o/a

Elcar; 1st o/a

Quip; 1st o/a *by 1 second!!!* with Phil Shaw

Cumbria; retired, crashed, with Sue

1983

Mintex; 12th o/a, with Billy Ballcock

York National; 11th o/a, with Billy Ballcock

Lampton Park; 2nd o/a

Haspengow; retired head gasket, with Half a Brain

Sold NWR 184V to Pete Slights

1984

York National; retired, oil leak with Lou Naylor *in PSG 461P Mk. 2 bought from Wales – BDG Terry Hoyle engine from John Brown*

Hadrian; retired can't remember why.

Champions Oliver's Mount; 3rd o/a

Severn Valley; 4th o/a, with Codpiece

Wombleton; 1st o/a

Border (Gallashiels); retired oil bung, with Codpiece

Quip; 8th o/a, with Billy Ballcock

Oulton Park; 1st o/a, with Codpiece

Knowsley; 5th o/a, with Codpiece

Sherwood Norking; 6th (puncture)

1985

National Breakdown; retired head gasket, with Billy Ballcock

York National; 7th o/a ignition wire, with Tony Coatsworth

Tour of Hamsterley; retired (log pile).......*with Codpiece – "Oh fuck! He did tell me."*

Welsh; retired half shaft, with Billy Ballcock

Cadwell Park; 3rd o/a in the race. *Sold PSG to don't know who! Maybe broke the car up…..*

New car – HRS 394V – blue Mk. 2 bought from Mick Redford

Premier; lying 3rd o/a until broken half shaft, with Cod Eye

Quip; 7th o/a with Cod Eye

Cadwell Park rally; 3rd o/a, with Rocket

Oulton Park rally; 3rd o/a (wheels loose), with Rocket

Acaster Malbis; 6th o/a, with Willybobs

Sherwoods of Darlington, Northallerton Stages; 1st o/a, with Rocket

1986

Tour of Lincs; 1st o/a with Billy Ballcock (Dave Elcock)

Cadwell Park race; 1st o/a

Hamsterley; retired (head gasket), with Billy Ballcock

Oliver's Mount; 1st o/a, with Billy Ballcock

Mallory Park race; 4th o/a

Severn Valley; retired on 2 cylinders, with Billy Ballcock

Yuk buys GJN 126T fitted with fuel injection

Croft Stages; 1st o/a with Rocket

Donnington race; 3rd o/a – won't rev

Plains Rally; 18th o/a, with Alf, drowned out in Myherin

Border Rally; 8th o/a (broken half shaft)

Quip Stages; 13th o/a, with Alf

Wolds Rally, Mablethorpe; 1st o/a with Rocket

Donington Stages; 2nd o/a, with Rocket

Premier Stages; 1st o/a, with Billy Ballcock

Donington single venue again; 1st o/a, with Susie

Cadwell Rally; 1st o/a, with Willibobs

1987

National Breakdown; retired head gasket

York National; 11th o/a with Billy Ballcock, misted up and small off

Plains Rally; 11th o/a puncture

Mallory Park race; 4th o/a

Tour of Hamsterley; with Phil Shaw 3rd o/a, brakes issue

Oulton Park race; loose wheel *new engine fitted 2.1 from Millington*

Donegal; retired broken crown wheel and pinion, on 48 Webbers

Nicolet; 2nd o/a, with Andy Moss

Border; retired rotor arm, with Andy Moss

Silva Stages; 2nd o/a, with Andy Moss

Sold car to Jason Humble with HRS plate.

Bought Opel Manta 400 WIA 5958 from Pete Slights

Quip Rally; 26th o/a, with Pete Slights

Wolds Stages; 2nd o/a, with Andy Moss

Cambrian; retired crashed when lying 9th, with Andy Moss

Crystal Stages; 2nd o/a, with Andy Moss

Cadwell Park Rally; 4th o/a, with Sus

Christmas Stages; 6th o/a, with Bilko

1988

National Breakdown Trophy Rally; 2nd o/a, with Billy Ballcock

York National; 7th o/a, with Amos

Plains; 13th o/a puncture

Des Winks Wombleton Airfield; 1st o/a, with Alison Stansfield

Hamsterley; 5th o/a 1st in class with Sus

Oliver's Mount; 12th o/a after off for 3 mins with Bottles

Kerridge Severn Valley; retired dust! New engine, with Alf

Oulton Park race; retired fire exting. went off!

Wombleton Airfield; 1st o/a, with Kate Richardson

Cadwell Rally; off for two and half mins. due to ice on 2nd stage! With Amos

1989

Cartel Trophy Rally; 2nd o/a, with Alan Moss

York National; retired, head gasket

Sylva Stages; 13th o/a off for 3mins with Amos

Border; with Amos

Sold Manta to Brian Price in South Wales

Bought G3 from Martyn Harrison

Crystal; retired water in plug, with Alan Andrews

Hamsterley; 4th o/a, with Alan Andrews

Cambrian; retired compression strut fell off, with Alan Andrews

Melbourne Airfield; 4th o/a, with Alan Andrews

Cadwell Park; retired, with Alan Andrews

1990

National Breakdown; retired, with Alan Andrews

Hadrian; 27th handling issues, with Alf

Summer Stages; 4th o/a, with Alan Andrews

Hamsterley; retired with broken rack, with Alan Andrews

Autocross, Hunmanby; 2nd o/a

Bought Mk. 3 Escort with Mk. 2 floor pan

Norking Alcan; retired broken caliper with Alan Andrews

Everyhope Hamsterley; 8th o/a, with Craig Thorley

Barkston Clubmans; 1st overall, with Ginge (screen wash in helmet!)

Crystal; retired with core plug issues, with Alan Andrews

Lookout Stages, Melbourne; retired head gasket with Sus

Kwik Fix Cadwell; 6th o/a with Christine Parling

Christmas Stages, retired in deep snow with Peter Croft
Nov. 1990 Jem born!!!

1991

Talkland Trophy Stages; 3rd o/a, dark and road penalties!!!, with Ginge
Lakeland; 6th o/a after puncture, with Willybobs (Adrian Wilson)
York National; 12th o/a 1st in class, with Ginge (Nigel Cay)
Plains; 12th o/a with Peter Croft
Hadrian; 15th o/a with Peter Croft
Summer Stages; retired broken starter
Built new Mk. 2, GJN with 2.2 Millington Diamond from Martin Thomas
Quinton; 14th o/a, with Mark Wareham
Silva Stages; retired, siezed hub, with Mark Wareham
Border; 16th o/a, *too many Jocks!*, with Peter Croft
Shell Oils Cumbria; won Trophy, with Peter Croft
Norking; 3rd o/a with Crofty
Barkston; 2nd o/a with Crofty
Crystal; 4th o/a with Crofty
Jersey Rally; retired, got lost with Handbag!
Cambrian; 15th o/a with Crofty
Melbourne; 2nd o/a and Spirit of the Rally with Billy Split Pin (first event for Billy!)
Cadwell; 1st o/a

1992

Wydean; 5th o/a with Peter Croft
Lakeland; 2nd o/a with PC
Langbaurgh Rallycross
Tour of Lincs; 3rd o/a, with PC
Hadrian Centurion; 10th o/a, with Billy Split Pin
Seizoen Rally; 7th o/a, with PC
Donegal; retired pedal box problems, with PC
Plains; 23rd o/a, lots of rain, with PC
Changed Mk. 2 from blue to yellow
Quinton; 11th o/a problems with alternator, with PC

Border; 9th o/a, with PC

Bushwacker; DFK!!!!, with PC

Crystal; 4th o/a 1st 2wd with PC

Cambrian; 4th o/a, with PC

Christmas Stages; 8th o/a, icy and hung over, with PC

BTRDA Championship 7th o/a

Stripped and sold car to Craig McIntosh

1993

Bought BMW EXI 1465 from John Price.

Belguim Seizoen Rally; 9th o/a, with Peter Croft

Donegal; retired alternator earth, with Peter Croft

Manby; retired with misfire, with PC

Charlemagne; 13th o/a, with PC

Quinton; 32nd, fucked rear tyres in 10 miles and delayed with car off, with Mark Wareham

Silva Stages; 5th till exhaust bust, with Paul Howarth

Yellow Brick Road; 32nd maximum on Airfield, with Mark Wareham.

Elvington; retired while leading, with Billy Split Pin

Flanders; crashed, *that fucked it!!!!*

1994

BMW re-shelled

Yellow Brick Road; retired loose wire, Nick Kennedy

Woodpecker; retired with throttle pot issues, with Julia Rabbett

Artemis; retired halfshaft, with John Birkett

Cambrian; retired with loose diff, with Wilf Pickles

Midland; 13th o/a, with Baz Dove

Wombleton; 5th o/a wet and shitty with Jon Birkett

Crystal; 18th with Jon

Melbourne Course car, with Jon, retired with fuel pressure issues

Cadwell; 3rd o/a with Ann Watson

1995

Riponian; retired with broken prop, with Billy Split Pin

Kall Kwik; Piggy drove car to 3rd o/a with Billy Split Pin, I did my back in!

North Humberside; 42nd, 5th in class. Puncture, was lying 13th, with Billy Split Pin

Pirelli; 2nd o/a, with Jim Kitson

Plains; retired with fuel pressure problems, with Craig Thorley

Des Winks Stages, Wombleton; retired broken half shaft, with Paul Skinner

Cadwell; 6th o/a, with Paul Skinner.

1996

Christmas Stages, Croft; 4th o/a, with Billy Split Pin

Crystal; 10th o/a, shitty roads with Willybobs

Donegal; retired when diff fell out on 3rd day, with Matt Whattam

Armstrong Massey; retired with driveshaft failure, with Matt Whattam.

Sold BMW to Melvyn Evans p/x for Rothmans livered Mk. 2 with 2.2 Millington Diamond

1997

Lookout Stages; 3rd o/a, very wet, with Terry Wilson

Donegal; 30th o/a, 2nd in class, with Dudley Dave

Charlemagne; retired clutch and puncture, with Terry Wilson

Sold Rothmans coloured Escort to John Dalton

1998

Built a new Mk. 2 for Donegal, sold to Hamish in Inverness.

Donegal; retired 3rd stage with broken gearbox, with Jim Kitson

1999

Built new Mk. 1

Tour of Lincs; retired tired(!), with Bill Haley (Steve McNulty)

Melbourne; 13th o/a tyres rubbish, with Steve McNulty

Silverstone Sprint

Donegal; 3 cylinders and broken gearstick, with Dave Robson

Armstrong Massey; oil belt broke, with Steve McNulty

Crystal; retired dropped valve.

2000 to 2006

Nowt going on much rallying wise!

2007

Built Mk. I Escort with Honda engine XTW 868L
Malton Rally; 34th o/a with misfire, with Jem
Kall Kwik; 8th o/a, with Jem

2008

Jack Frost; misfire and penalties for a short cut, with Jem
Riponian; 4 spins, lost gears, with Joe Cruttens
Humberside; retired with broken box, with Jem
Chatsworth Rally Show; 2nd in class, with Jem
Dukeries; 56th o/a 5th in class, stopped on stage
Greystoke; 16th o/a, with Jem
Trackrod; 14th o/a, with Jem
Croft Track Day
Malton Rally; 37 o/a, very wet, been in ditch x 3, with Jem
Kall Kwik; 14th o/a 3rd in class, dark but no spins!
Christmas Stages; damaged thumb and had flu, with Jem

2009

Riponian; 30th o/a 6th in class, with Jem
Bought Millington Diamond motor off a transvestite on EBay! Built into Gartrac Mk. 2 shell bought from Ireland
Greystoke; retired 3/4 mile in on first stage with busted crank! *Bollocks!*

2010

Lookout Stages; Melbourne retired rota arm, with Jem
Hamsterley; 31 st o/a, with Jem
John Everard, Melbourne; retired engine mount, with Billy Split Pin
Chatsworth Rally Show; retired valve seat, with Jem
Malton Rally; non started with distributer probs., with Jem

2011

Riponian; 28th o/a, snow, spins and 3 offs! with Jonboy.

Border; retired 2nd stage with duff alternator, with Jem

Hamsterley; 28th o/a, broken stick, starter, penalties and limp mode, with Jem

Birkbecks; Single venue, retired half shaft

Trackrod; retired punctures, with Jem

Malton; 25th o/a, bent steering arm, with Jem

2012

Christmas Stages; retired oil cooler, with Billy Split Pin

Byton Airfield Rally Charity Day

Trackrod; punctured, retired not classified, with Billy Split Pin.

Croft Roger Albert Clark Rally Press Day

2013

Christmas Stages; retired with severe misfire, with JP

Approximate number of events (lots forgotten about!) = 300 Plus!

So, how did you get the name Yuk?

We were on the Greystoke Rally one year at signing on and we were having a bit of banter with a few people. One of the women in the signing on team asked me how I got to be called Yuk.

Later on as we came in to service, Pearl Wilson (Malcolm Wilson's mum) comes up to me and says that she had been talking to someone. "My friend at signing on says we've had this funny, little grey-haired fella, who says he's Chinese, come on the rally." Pearl says, "He's not Chinese, he's Yuk from York!"